Cambridge Elements ≡

Elements in Politics and Society in Southeast Asia
edited by
Edward Aspinall
Australian National University
Meredith L. Weiss
University at Albany, SUNY

GENDER IN SOUTHEAST ASIA

Mina Roces
University of New South Wales, Sydney

CAMBRIDGE
UNIVERSITY PRESS

University Printing House, Cambridge CB2 8BS, United Kingdom

One Liberty Plaza, 20th Floor, New York, NY 10006, USA

477 Williamstown Road, Port Melbourne, VIC 3207, Australia

314–321, 3rd Floor, Plot 3, Splendor Forum, Jasola District Centre,
New Delhi – 110025, India

103 Penang Road, #05–06/07, Visioncrest Commercial, Singapore 238467

Cambridge University Press is part of the University of Cambridge.

It furthers the University's mission by disseminating knowledge in the pursuit of
education, learning, and research at the highest international levels of excellence.

www.cambridge.org
Information on this title: www.cambridge.org/9781108741637
DOI: 10.1017/9781108680493

First published 2022

A catalogue record for this publication is available from the British Library.

ISBN 978-1-108-74163-7 Paperback
ISSN 2515-2998 (online)
ISSN 2515-298X (print)

Gender in Southeast Asia

Elements in Politics and Society in Southeast Asia

DOI: 10.1017/9781108680493
First published online: February 2022

Mina Roces
University of New South Wales, Sydney

Author for correspondence: Mina Roces, m.roces@unsw.edu.au

Abstract: This Element examines gender in Southeast Asia by focusing on two main themes. The first concerns hegemonic cultural constructions of gender and Southeast Asian subjects' responses to these dominant discourses. Four sections are devoted to: first, discussing hegemonic discourses on ideal masculinities and ideal femininities; second, evaluating the impact of religion; third, analysing how authoritarian regimes fashion these ideals; and, fourth, explaining hegemonic ideals surrounding desire and sexualities and the way these are policed by society and the state. The second theme is on how hegemonic ideals influence the gendering of power and politics. I argue that because many Southeast Asians see power as being held by the kinship alliance group and not just the person in office, women are able to access political power through their ties with men – as wives, mothers, daughters, sisters and even mistresses. Women's movements have challenged this androcentric division of power.

Keywords: gender; women; Southeast Asia, sexualities; masculinity; femininity; politics

ISBNs: 9781108741637 (PB), 9781108680493 (OC)
ISSNs: 2515-2998 (online), 2515-298X (print)

Contents

1 Introduction

1.1 Themes

Southeast Asia is a rich and complex site for carrying out research in gender studies, as each country poses its own contradictions in the struggle for gender equality. For example, the Philippines is the only Asian country to have made the top ten in the 2018 Global Gender Gap Report (meaning to say it is one of the best countries in the world in terms of gender equality already achieved), but it is also one of just two or three countries in the world where absolute divorce is not legally possible. In Malaysia, hegemonic cultural constructions of gender see men as "reason" and women as "passion," but not when it comes to financial matters, where men are imagined to be more susceptible to squandering money on gambling, alcohol or women (Peletz 1996; 1995). These two examples reveal the trials that both scholars and gender activists working in this field face as they try to make sense of the complexities of cultural constructions of gender in specific Southeast Asian countries. The intersections of class, ethnicity, cultural contexts and unique postcolonial histories make it difficult to identify a singular national, let alone Southeast Asia-wide, construction of the feminine and the masculine (Ikeya 2014: 250). This enormous challenge is made more complex by the fact that these constructs are not static and change over time. The intersectional differences of class and ethnicity also matter. But the diversity of cultural, religious and political contexts in Southeast Asia makes it a fertile place for analyzing gender differences that both defy and modify dominant paradigms that emanate from the Western world.

This Element examines the vast topic of gender in the region from around the 1950s and 1960s until 2020, focusing on two main themes. The first concerns hegemonic cultural constructions of gender and Southeast Asian subjects' responses (including resistance) to them. Four sections are devoted to discussing: first, hegemonic discourses on ideal masculinities and ideal femininities (Section 2); second, the role of religion in influencing these ideals (Section 3); third, how authoritarian governments have tried to fashion gender constructs to benefit state objectives (Section 4); and, fourth, hegemonic ideals surrounding desire and sexualities and the way these are policed by society and the state (Section 5). The discussion of hegemonic ideals in each section is followed by examples of how activists and other groups have challenged or resisted these ideals, and proposed alternative gender constructs, zeroing in on processes of change and contests over gender norms throughout the region. The theme of cultural constructions of gender is extremely important because it acts as an umbrella for a huge corpus of scholarship in the field and informs the starting point for many research questions dealing with gender issues in the region.

These social constructions inform myriad gender roles, including what is classified as women's work and responsibilities, as well as articulating the criteria for policing appropriate behavior for each gender. The body of work that studies women's movements, for example, has had to confront constructions of gender in some form or another in order to begin to understand how activists have tried to dismantle these ideals. It is for these reasons that I have chosen to ground this study in an overview of this topic.

The second theme explored in the volume concerns hegemonic ideals influencing the gendering of power and politics in the region, which is the focus of Section 6. I argue that because widely shared concepts of power in Southeast Asia understand power as being held by the kinship alliance group and not just the person in office, women are frequently able to access political power through their ties with men – as wives, mothers, daughters, sisters and even mistresses. I use the term *kinship alliance group* because this category includes not just kin, but also persons such as employees and close friends who, due to their personal ties with the person in office, would be perceived to have the power to influence that individual (Roces 1998: 2, 8–19). In politics, women often exercise power through their ties with male politicians, and behind the scenes. I am not merely claiming that kinship is important to politics, or that there are gendered roles in the kinship group. What I am arguing here is that Southeast Asian concepts of power empower women in ways that are not possible in Western societies. The implication is that since women can hold unofficial power behind the scenes through links with male politicians, one can argue that politics in Southeast Asia is at least less male-dominated than it would appear at first sight. However, the argument also suggests that women's power is often still linked to women's supportive (rather than leadership) roles in the kinship group. At the end of Section 6, I discuss how women's movements have challenged this androcentric division of power.

In presenting this Element, I underscore that these dominant discourses are extremely powerful and have been entrenched for a long time. They are enforced by social norms, by religious beliefs, by the strong arm of the state and by the kinship group. It is important to understand that the agency of women and subordinated sexualities is particularly limited in environments where absolute obedience of daughters and children is required, and transgression can result in family shame or social ostracism. The consequences of social exclusion in societies where personal ties are extremely important make it difficult for activists to resist, challenge or break taboos. At the same time, if one grows up in an environment where one's social reality is tightly controlled (especially in authoritarian regimes) it is difficult to imagine alternative gender constructs. As a Filipino woman brought up in the Philippines and who is still quite connected there, I have myself experienced discrimination and censure for not living up to the ideal of becoming a wife and mother, and I appreciate the courage needed to face the scorn of relatives and former classmates who see me as a failure. On the other hand, my situation as a migrant in Australia has given me the opportunity to critically reflect on these cultural constructs. However, my many conversations with Filipino women in the homeland and abroad (Roces 2021) remind me of the limits of women's agency. Activists – both feminist activists and LGBT advocates – also have transnational links with global movements. Thus, their gender theorizing is transnationally produced (Roces 2010: 1–20) and their links with the international gender movements give them more agency in the campaign for change. In fact, the Philippines arguably hosts one of the most robust women's movements in the world (Roces 2012), although the same cannot be said about most Southeast Asian countries.

1.2 Scholarship on Gender in Southeast Asia

The study of gender in Southeast Asia is a strong and vigorous field of scholarship. It is, however, quite uneven. While the topic of "women in Asia" is a field in its own right, with regular conferences, journals and book series, there is only a tiny handful of publications about heterosexual masculinity. To date only one edited volume addresses men and masculinities in Southeast Asia (Ford and Lyons 2011), compared to the many anthologies on women in Asia. As that pioneering volume laments, there is a lack of studies of men as "gendered beings" (Ford and Lyons 2011: 1). Moreover, Lyn Parker (2008) says: "at present we have the rather bizarre situation that we seem to have more explicit and sophisticated work on alternative sexualities than we do on hegemonic heterosexuality"; Ford and Lyons 2011). This observation is echoed by Chie Ikeya, as follows.

> Masculinity as an analytical concept has received limited attention in historical and cultural studies of Asia, particularly of South and Southeast Asia. Only a number of works produced in South and Southeast Asian studies address the historical construction and evolution of masculinities in the regions, and even fewer present in-depth inquiries into the extent to which historical forms of masculinity govern social relations. The specific dynamics of the relationship between ideologies and the interpretation, experience and performance of manhood in daily life, both in the past and in present times, remain underexplored. (Ikeya 2014: 244)

The literature is also dominated by the discipline of anthropology, although historians have also made significant contributions on gender histories from the precolonial period to the present. In addition, the fields of literature, film and cultural studies have also produced important works on the way gender is represented in popular culture and major literary texts.

In this short survey I will concentrate on three pioneering anthologies that have tackled the topic of cultural constructions of gender in the entire region. I have chosen them because they have not only opened new ground in the project of researching cultural constructions of gender, but because they have also provoked scholars to think about how the Southeast Asian contexts present us with new ways of thinking about the gendering of power, politics, prestige systems and potency, or else have alerted us to the contradictions and complexities in the official gender discourses found in the region.

In 1991, Maila Stivens' edited book *Why Gender Matters in Southeast Asian Politics* was the first to critique the androcentric scholarship in the discipline of political science, suggesting that the question is "not so much why gender matters in Southeast Asian politics but why gender has not been seen to matter by political science in the region" (Stivens 1991: 24). This book not only exposes the invisibility of women in the major monographs in that discipline, but also mounts a convincing case for the need to expand the view of politics to reveal the way women have been important political actors in the region (Stivens 1991). It also suggests that one way forward would be to link up Southeast Asian studies with "feminism and the theoretical analysis of state relations," but with the caveat that Western feminist theories should not be grafted unproblematically onto the Southeast Asian context (Stivens 1991: 8–24).

A major pioneering work in the discipline of anthropology situates "gender" as a primary topic for analysis in Southeast Asian societies. Atkinson and Errington's *Power and Difference: Gender in Island Southeast Asia* (1990) theorizes the gender status and prestige system through the prism of "spiritual potency", arguing that status in the region is measured by spiritual potency, including the ability to attract an audience, accumulate and display wealth or connect with the spirit world as shamans (Errington 1990: 41–53). Women, they argue, "tend to be less successful collectors of potency than men" (Errington 1990: 46) and this has an enormous impact on their social and political status so that, for example, a woman who became a shaman in Wana (Central Sulawesi, Indonesia) society was someone who had beaten the odds (Atkinson 1990: 83).

In 1995, Aihwa Ong and Michael G. Peletz published *Bewitching Women, Pious Men: Gender and Body Politics in Southeast Asia* (Ong and Peletz 1995). This anthology was the first to analyze the contradictions in hegemonic cultural constructions of gender in several Southeast Asian contexts. The example I used in the opening paragraph of this Element, in which Michael Peletz discusses how in Malaysia men are constructed as "reason" and women as "passion," appears here (see also Peletz 1996). Suzanne Brenner's chapter proposes a similar argument. She argues that Javanese women dominate the marketplace because men are imagined to be incapable of controlling their passions when it comes to financial matters, whereas women are seen to be adept at finances. On the other hand, female autonomy in the marketplace means that they lose status as bargaining involves behavior that lowers their spiritual potency (Brenner 1995: 26–50).

Almost three decades have passed since the publication of these seminal studies and since then a plethora of publications on women in Southeast Asia have appeared – so much so that "gender" until recently stood for the category of "women" in literature on the region. Southeast Asian women are no longer invisible in political science, anthropology, history, the social sciences, media, literature and film, and cultural studies. Today, we have the problem of imbalance in the scholarship, where studies on women far outnumber those on men and masculinities.

The scholarship to date can be grouped into several thematic strands. Though they grapple with various topics, many of them engage in one way or another with cultural constructions of gender. Due to the limits of language and research expertise, most studies are country-focused rather than region-focused and attempts at transnational studies come in collaborative works in the form of anthologies or edited volumes. Women's activism and gender activism (on behalf of LGBT groups, for example) is well documented in the region (Edwards and Roces 2004; Roces and Edwards 2010; Blackburn 2004; Lyons 2004; Lee 2018; Ng et al. 2006; Martyn 2005; Basarudin 2016; Wijaya 2020; Chua 2018; Coloma 2013; Tang 2017). The topic of women and politics is also a popular focus, especially for anthologies on the region (Roces 1998; Jacobsen 2008; Iwanaga 2008; Derichs and Thompson 2013; Dewi 2015; Devasayaham 2019). Historians have made a contribution by analyzing gender in the precolonial and postcolonial eras (Andaya 2000; 2001; 2008; Reyes and Clarence-Smith 2012; Ikeya 2011; Reyes 2008; Taylor 1997). Other themes that have frequently been addressed by scholars working across several geographical areas are the topics of women, work and the marketplace (Sen and Stivens 1998; Ford and Parker 2008; Brenner 1998; Leshkowich 2014; Wolf 1992; Ong 1987; Baird et al. 2017), prostitution (Sandy 2014; Jeffrey 2001; Murray 1991), women and migration (Parreñas 2001; Lan 2006), motherhood (Stivens 1996); women's health (Whittaker 2000; 2004), representations of women/gender in film and literature (Sears 1996; Murtagh 2013; Creese 2004), gender and sexualities (mostly focusing on women and subordinated sexualities) (Bennett 2005; Bennett and Davies 2015; Blackwood 2010; Boellstorff 2005; Davies 2007; 2010; Garcia 1996; Jackson 1995; 2011; Jackson and Cook 1999; Jackson and Sullivan 1999; Sinnott 2004; Wilson 2004; Wieringa 2015), gender and the state's fashioning of gender ideals in specific time periods (O'Shaughnessy

2009; Pettus 2003; Robinson 2018; Suryakusuma 1996; Werner 2009; Werner and Bélanger 2002) and gender and religion (with most works focusing on women and religion) (Endres 2011; Falk 2007; 2009; Kawanami 2013; Kloos 2019; Nurmila 2009; Smith and Woodward 2014; Smith-Hefner 2019; Van Wichelen 2010). There is now also a growing body of work on youth in the disciplines of anthropology, sociology and education (Downing 2019; Hefner 2019; Joseph 2014; Parker and Nilan 2013; Rydstrom 1998; Smith-Hefner 2019). Social scientists (mainly anthropologists) continue to dominate the field, especially in studies of both ethnic minorities and class, but there are many anthologies which are truly interdisciplinary. There are countries or geographical areas which have inspired a plethora of published work. Indonesia leads the pack with the Philippines, Thailand, Malaysia, Vietnam, Singapore and Myanmar also coming in close, while others such as Laos, Brunei and East Timor have been given less attention (with the exception of Niner 2016 and Creak 2015). In Section 7 of this Element, I discuss the scholarship's contribution to gender studies generally, and the areas for future research.

2 Gender Ideals

2.1 Introduction

Throughout Southeast Asia, the hegemonic gender ideal for men is as bread-winner, warrior or political and religious leader. The hegemonic gender ideal for women as the Other of men is that of wife and mother. This section will discuss the overarching dominant discourses that define the masculine and the feminine in Southeast Asia and activists' attempts to critique them, dismantle them and propose alternative ideals. In this section I examine hegemonic discourses regarding men and women's roles in the family and in the household economic unit. Then I discuss the ways Southeast Asian feminists have produced their own gender theorizing and the strategies they deploy in their long-term project of modifying hegemonic ideals in order to empower women.

2.2 Ideal Men and Ideal Women

According to dominant gender discourses throughout Southeast Asia, the ideal man is a "pillar of the family" or the head of the household responsible for family decisions (though women typically handle the finances) (Harriden 2012; Parreñas 2005: 57; Leshkowich 2014: 70). In Singapore, the principle that men are the heads of households was used by the government as a guiding principle for policies particularly in the mid-1980s, and removing this discriminatory discourse has been one major rallying cry for the feminist movement there (Chan 2000; Lyons 2010). Men do not do domestic work and any contribution they make to childcare, for example, is acceptable only if it is interpreted as merely "helping out" (Hoang and Yeoh 2011: 720; Parreñas 2005). As Hoang and Yeoh eloquently put it, with reference to Vietnam: "doing household labor is equated with doing gender: women do it and men do not" (Hoang and Yeoh 2011: 729). The most important masculine attribute for a married man is that of being the breadwinner. Married men must be good economic providers for their families (Pingol 2001: 8, 33 and 223). The requirement that husbands and fathers must be good providers is so intrinsic to constructions of masculinity throughout Southeast Asia that men who cannot fulfill this ideal at home often seek jobs overseas (Jacobsen 2012; McKay and Lucero-Prismo III 2012). Filipino seafarers, even those in the lower ranks of the elaborate hierarchy on a maritime vessel, earn in US dollars much more than the average worker in the Philippines and as such are held up as ideal men, epitomizing "breadwinner masculinity" not just because they are exemplary providers, but also because of the sacrifices they make in the pursuit of "responsible fatherhood" (McKay and Lucero-Prismo 2012: 20–21). In Myanmar, if women earn money, most people accept this only so long as it is meant only to be supplementary income (Harriden 2012: 147).

In Southeast Asian hegemonic discourses the feminine ideal is as "wife and mother". A woman is defined by her attachments to a man (a father, a husband or a son), and her role is connected with her relationship with men (Sears 1996: 19 on Indonesian women) as a wife, mother, sister or daughter. While it is true that men are sometimes introduced as sons of a prominent father, for example, they are generally able to establish individual identities as leaders in the secular and religious spheres, as workers or as career professionals. A man who never marries may be seen as outside the norm, but he does not suffer the same level of discrimination that a single woman past marriageable age experiences. On the other hand, most Southeast Asians generally define women according to their kinship roles. In Cambodia, "it is not surprising that the categories of single woman and prostitute should be so linked, as there has never been a socially acceptable place for women outside of the family roles of daughter, wife or mother" (Frieson 2001: 6). Women who have never married (spinsters) and women who are divorced or are widows experience terrible discrimination (see Section 5). One exception may be Myanmar. Many Burmese admire spinsters, who are known as *apyogyi* or "big virgins" for their commitment to celibacy. These women are able to develop professional careers, claim economic independence and gain status from their donations to the Buddhist monkhood (Harriden 2012: 35). However, as a rule the dominant view is that a single woman past marriageable age is pitied because she has failed to fulfill her destiny as a woman.

The ideal also requires women to be dutiful or obedient daughters, and chaste and faithful wives. In countries which have Confucian influence, such as Vietnam, "women must observe the three obediences (*tam tòng*) to father, husband, and eldest son, and the four virtues (*tứ đức*) of capable work (*công*), decorous appearance (*dung*), polite speech (*ngôn*), and deferential behavior (hanh)" (Leshkowich 2014: 14–15). Women must also be virtuous and pious. In Cambodia the ideal woman's required list of virtues is enshrined in the text of the *Chbap Srei* (*Rules for Women*), first written at the turn of the nineteenth century and taught to Cambodians at home and in school (Jacobsen 2008: 75ff). The ideal Cambodian woman is the *srey kruap leak* or "perfectly virtuous woman" who is soft-spoken, walks quietly, speaks sweetly to her husband, sits modestly and does not draw attention to herself (Ledgerwood 1996: 142–43; Bricknell 2011: 437–38). Filipino coming-of-age celebrations for girls turning eighteen (known as "debuts" in the Philippines) even among the diaspora underscore these hegemonic cultural constructions of the feminine as obedient and chaste daughters (Rodriguez 2012). Women are also expected to be bearers and wearers of national tradition. In national celebrations such as Kartini Day in Indonesia, women wear the *sarong kebaya* (the national dress of a wrapped *batik* skirt and long-sleeved blouse) and the Singapore Girl, attired in *sarong kebaya*, is heralded as the iconic brand of Singapore Airlines.

At the same time, women are typically in charge of the household purse strings and are responsible for the family budget. Across the region, husbands are supposed to surrender their pay packets to their wives, who give them a little allowance for their leisure pursuits such as alcohol or cigarettes (Leshkowich 2014: 13; Brenner 1998). The Vietnamese phrase "generals of the interior" captures this view (Leshkowich 2014: 13). While Western liberal feminists might see this as evidence for women in this region having more financial independence and autonomy, Southeast Asian feminists have argued that this responsibility is an enormous burden, especially for women of the lower classes who have to think in creative ways to extend the purchasing power of their husbands' measly paychecks (Roces 2012; Harriden 2012: 19). Likewise, anthropologists have alerted us to the fact that prestige and status in Southeast Asia are also influenced by concepts of spiritual potency, and that women's association with money matters therefore lowers rather than raises their cultural capital (Brenner 1998). In Theravada Buddhist countries like Thailand and Myanmar, where societies are preoccupied with accumulating good karma (called "merit" or *bun* in Thai), the woman's responsibility for the family's financial budget places her at a lower status than the man because she is concerned with material things – a this-worldly preoccupation (Falk 2007). In Java, women dominate the marketplace as vendors and customers. In this public sphere the custom of haggling or bargaining over each item is crucial for the performance of women's roles as managers of the family's economic resources. This practice requires women to raise their voices in conflict. Such a spectacle of greed and materialism demeans women's prestige by showing a lack of refinement and results in being considered low-status (Brenner 1998: 140). Thus, women's behavior in the marketplace locates them in the low-status category of "coarse" (*kasar*) conduct in a society where refinement and self-control are held in esteem (Brenner 1998: 140–70).

Similarly, in Vietnam (from the post-1989 Renovation Era when the country introduced market-oriented policies), the marketplace is considered the woman's domain due to essentialized constructions of women as "naturally" good traders (Leshkowich 2014: 4–5). Selling goods at the market is one acceptable profession for women since this business is considered as being "on the side" or "supplementary" to women's primary role as wives and mothers (Leshkowich, 2014: 71). Even so, Vietnamese consider women's trading activity to be selfish and immoral because bargaining involves an element of duplicity. This process of haggling, which Vietnamese call the art of "talking nonsense" (e.g., using flattery to convince a customer to buy one's goods, lowering one's status as a strategy to attract potential buyers), if deployed by a male would lower his prestige (Leshkowich 2014: 64–66). Such blatant display of a lack of virtue places women lower than men in the moral hierarchy (Leshkowich 2014: 15). The irony of it all is that trading actually brings in more lucrative profits than the higher-status but lower-pay civil service jobs men possess (Leshkowich 2014). Since trading is so closely aligned with women, men who enter this world are faced with the quandary of having to present themselves as incompetent traders, rather than as successful businessmen, in order to preserve their masculinity (Leshkowich 2014: 74).

One of the most striking aspects of gender paradigms in Southeast Asia is that contradictory discourses can exist side by side. Javanese assume that their men are better than women at accumulating spiritual potency (one index of status and power in Javanese society), since women's attention to financial matters results in the aggressive haggling expected of them in the marketplace: behavior considered *kasar* and by definition lacking in spiritual potency. However, there is an alternative discourse that men have less self-control in spending money because Javanese believe they are more likely to succumb to lust and vices such as gambling (Brenner 1995; 1998). In Thailand and Cambodia a man who shows virility and sexual potency is admired, but so is the ascetic ideal epitomized by the Buddhist monk (Keeler 2017; Jacobsen 2012: 86–102). These contradictory discourses – which remain in flux – demonstrate the complexities involved in analyzing representations of gender in the region.

Throughout Southeast Asia there is space in traditional societies for variations from the gender binary. The *bissu* of South Sulawesi are androgynous shamans – they are both male and female, part-human and part-deity – and therefore potent beings able to communicate with the spirit world (Davies 2007: 6–102; Andaya 2000: 38). But a true *bissu* "must refrain from any type of sexual activity and even lustful desire of any earthly thing" and may not expel bodily fluid such as semen or menstrual blood (Davies 2007: 90). If they break these strict rules of ascetism they are punished (Davies 2007: 90). The *bissu* are potent beings able to conduct rituals but considered asexual. In this sense they identify as a separate gender from male and female.[1]

Social economic changes themselves can also influence hegemonic constructs. One of the consequences of the feminization of migration is the transformation of women into breadwinners, earning more than their husbands in overseas contract employment. Alicia Pingol's seminal study of the left-behind "househusbands" reveals that men who are financially dependent on their wives' remittances feel threatened since this situation undermines what they know to be their fundamental role as husbands (Pingol 2001: 33). There are signs that the transnational family (i.e., a family with spouses separated for periods of time because of their overseas contract work) is becoming the reality for close to 10 percent of Filipinos who are migrant workers, and this has an impact on gender constructs as women become breadwinners. While Rhacel Parreñas' findings reveal that left-behind husbands usually delegate the domestic and caregiving work and responsibilities to female relatives, Pingol's study on the other hand found evidence that, although some men who feel they have failed the gender ideal may drown their sorrows in alcohol, gambling or womanizing, there are signs that others are remaking masculinity by embracing their new roles as "househusbands," learning to cook and care for children while the wives take on overseas contract work (Parreñas 2005; Pingol 2001).

2.3 Critiquing Gender Ideals and Proposing New Ones

What Western feminists have labeled "second-wave feminism"[2] – a movement of activists challenging patriarchy and dominant cultural constructions of gender – appeared in Southeast Asia from the 1980s onwards. As part of this trend,

---

[1] The *bissu* are another gender category (Andaya 2000). In Section 5, in which I discuss subordinated sexualities, I examine the categories of gay, lesbian, transgender and bisexual individuals and their partners. These categories are also gender categories (hence Sharyn Graham Davies has subtitled one of her books *Five Genders among the Bugis in Indonesia*), but their identities also reflect sexualities as well. It is for this reason that I discuss them in the section on sexualities.

[2] In Southeast Asia the first-wave feminist movement focused on suffrage rights as women campaigned for the right to vote and run for political office (Edwards and Roces 2004; Blackburn 2004; Roces and Edwards 2010).

women's movements in Southeast Asia have developed their own indigenous brands of feminism in response to the critique that feminism is "Western" and therefore inapplicable to the regional context (Roces 2010). They have offered critiques of local cultural constructions of gender and proposed their own alternative gender ideals. In Southeast Asia, from the 1980s onwards these activists have tested several theoretical positions, attempting to approach the "woman question" from the perspective of "grassroots" women, even though most activists are from the middle classes. Plugged into the network of trans-national women's rights movements, these Southeast Asian women activists have also fought for reproductive rights, raised the problems of domestic violence, rape, incest, polygamy, divorce, sexualities, education, poverty, women's roles in the family, including responsibility for the family's finances, the issue of military sexual slavery during the Japanese Occupation in World War II, the problems of women in factories and the urban poor, as well as the problems of women from indigenous minority groups. Activists have framed their campaigns through the language and approach of human rights.

For example, an analysis of the Filipino construction of the feminine has been absolutely critical for the development of Filipino feminist theory. According to feminist Catholic nun Mary John Mananzan (of the Order of Saint Benedict), the Spanish friars from the colonial period imposed "the impossible model of the Virgin Mary as the ideal woman" (Mananzan 1987: 34). This image of the Virgin Mary focused on the obedient Mary of the Anunciation, or the Mater Dolorosa ("suffering mother"), endorsing the belief that "enduring is necessary" (*pagtitiis ang kailangan*) or, worse, that "forbearance and patience" (*pagtitiis at pasensya*) were the solution to the problem of domestic violence or a philandering husband (Mananzan 1987: 4; Fabella 1987, 1991: 166–7; Arriola 1989: 25; de Dios 1999: 157). Maria Clara, Juli and Sisa, all fictional characters from national hero Jose Rizal's nineteenth-century novels that inspired the Philippine revolution against Spain, also became the role models for both elite and lower-class women from about the end of the nineteenth century onwards. These characters were quiet, hardworking, obedient, self-sacrificing and submissive. Filipina feminists aspired to dismantle the suffering martyr as the female ideal and suggested alternative role models to take their places. Using analyses from feminist theology, feminist Catholic nuns sought to replace the image of the Mater Dolorosa with Mary as woman (Roces 2012: 46). Nuns also hoped to demythologize "suffering" to remove the status assigned to the woman as martyr (Roces 2012: 46).

One of the alternative role models whom feminists proposed to replace Maria Clara, Sisa and Juli was Gabriela Silang – the wife of Diego Silang, an Ilocana rebel who led a revolt against the Spaniards in the seventeenth century. Gabriela took leadership of her husband's revolt and was herself caught and hanged in Vigan on September 20, 1763. The most prominently known feminist women's organization named itself after her. GABRIELA (General Assembly Binding Women for Reforms, Integrity, Equality, Leadership and Action) has been the umbrella organization for a plethora of women, grouped into sectors such as peasant women, women workers and indigenous women, and which also has its own women's party. Other role models suggested by feminists included Lorena Barros (who founded the MAKIBAKA in the early 1970s, the first second-wave feminist organization in the Philippines, and who was killed in a military encounter in 1976), Liza Balando (a factory worker who was killed during a demonstration demanding higher wages in 1971) and Liliosa Hilao (a religious woman who helped victims of illegal detention (Roces 2012: 23–26)). Finally, Filipina feminists also created their own muse – the *babaylan*, or the pre-Hispanic priestess who had religious power and whom poet Mila Aguilar reinterpreted as an "old rebel" (Aguilar 2006: 173–74). The *babaylan* was a woman past childbearing age who was not just a religious leader but was considered an elder, a wise person. Feminists claimed to have preserved the spirit of the *babaylan* in their "dangerous collective memory" and constructed a psychological link with this mysterious type of woman (Mananzan 1994: viii; Mangahas and Llaguno 2006: 42).

Women's movements in Malaysia and Thailand have prioritized certain practical issues that they have identified as most pressing for their local "national" situation. In Thailand, the "good" woman and the "bad" woman are defined in terms of their relationship to the family. The hegemonic ideal is the woman who is a dutiful daughter, faithful wife and all-giving mother. In the 1980s, Sukanya Hantrakul tried to critique this good girl/bad girl divide by advocating that sex workers should be protected and receive the same rights as other Thai citizens. She proposed that society should not question the choices sex workers make. Instead, she suggested that activists focus on providing skills such as English language training (Falk 2010: 117). Influenced by a similar philosophy, the Thai non-governmental organization (NGO) EMPOWER (Education Means Protection of Women Engaged in Recreation) rejects society's view of the need to reform prostitutes (to turn them back into "good" women), hoping instead to address the practical needs of sex workers such as giving them AIDS and health education, language classes and career workshops (Falk 2010: 117).

Women's movements have been most successful in the sphere of spreading awareness of some of the most important issues facing women across the region. Activists have defined and debated key concepts in feminist vocabularies such as sexual harassment, anti-trafficking, spousal rape and violence against women, sexual diversity, lesbianism, abortion, reproductive rights and sexual rights. In doing so, they have effectively developed a feminist canon specific to their own societies. Activists have then aspired to disseminate these new ideas more broadly, as a first step in transforming cultural attitudes. To this end, they have launched a motley collection of educational campaigns in order to encourage citizens in their countries to rethink the role of women and gender constructs and to join their campaigns for gender equality. In the Philippines, GABRIELA, the Women's Media Circle and the Institute of Women's Studies at St. Scholastica's College produced radio programs in the vernacular, which aired in the 1990s to early 2000s, that were literally women's studies courses complete with modules that explained Filipino feminist theoretical positions, discussing major issues facing women (Roces 2012). Malaysia also had a radio station for women in 2005, WFM 88.1, and although it was led by men there were opportunities to broadcast feminist issues such as domestic violence and sexual crimes (Ng et al. 2006: 161). In 2000, the Women's Media Centre in Cambodia produced radio programs that educated women about their rights and about health issues including contraception (called "family planning"), and informed women where to get help if they became victims of violence (Jacobsen 2010: 217). In Myanmar "community classrooms" became an important venue for mentoring women and raising awareness and the RAINFALL Gender Study Group, which began as a reading club, offered training, workshops and public advocacy forums for women (Maber and Han 2018: 268–80).

Across Southeast Asia, activists since the late 1980 also mobilized women, including survivors of rape, trafficking, labor exploitation, domestic violence and sexual harassment. They encouraged these courageous survivors to attend gender conscientization seminars and transformed them into activists through participation in demonstrations, theatre as advocacy and the performance of oral testimonies (especially for survivors of military sexual slavery, infidelity and sexual violence) (Roces 2012). In Malaysia, the Women's Candidacy Initiative (WCI) in 1999 instigated a comic campaign in which a fictitious woman named Mak Bedah ("Aunty Bedah") showed up at election campaign rallies presenting candidates with a "shopping list" of issues the WCI wanted addressed (Lee 2018: 33–45). These initiatives revealed the boundless creativity of women activists and attested to their superb organizational skills. They also demonstrated that activists were aware that the feminist project of re-educating the populace to become gender-sensitive was a long-term one.

3 Religion

3.1 Introduction

In Sections 3 and 4, I discuss two forces which have had an enormous role in defining and policing gender ideals: religion and authoritarian states. One powerful institution that gender activists identify as the biggest challenge to their advocacy is orthodox religion. Religions have been crucial in fashioning hegemonic gender ideals in Southeast Asia, and these hegemonic ideals are difficult to dismantle or critique in places where conservative religious leaders (most often male) exert enormous symbolic and moral power. This means that activists who dare to challenge these hegemonic ideals risk being demonized and ostracized. Religious beliefs also influence what issues are considered "taboo," such as sex outside heterosexual marriage and abortion, where just breaking the silence becomes a formidable task. Even when activists succeed in pushing for legal reform that goes against the consensus of the religious hierarchy, such as the passage of the Reproductive Health Law in the Philippines, the long road to implementation can be delayed, blocked or sabotaged by an entrenched conservative religious hierarchy (Collantes 2018: 75–77).

In many parts of Southeast Asia, religion is intrinsic to the fashioning of hegemonic male and female role models. In Theravada Buddhist Thailand, the ideal son is one who enters the monkhood (even if temporarily) and in doing so transfers good karma to his parents. Hence, Thai men become masculine through ordination (Falk 2007: 34), and the ideal male is an ex-monk who is a householder (Keyes 1984: 223–41). Thus, activists have the task of not just reinterpreting religious texts to empower women; they also have to find a way to appeal to or convince the religious leadership and the rest of society to embrace the radical changes they propose. This section will analyze two religions – Theravada Buddhism in Thailand and Myanmar, and Islam in Indonesia – to examine the way hegemonic religious ideologies have privileged men over women in the hierarchy of beings, marginalizing women from positions of religious leadership. It will then show how activists have responded by reinterpreting religious scriptures with a feminist lens to empower women, while lobbing for a space for women in the top echelons of the religious hierarchy.

3.2 Religious Power: Men as Spiritual Leaders, Women as Laity

In Southeast Asia, according to dominant interpretations men still have a near-monopoly over spiritual power. In Theravada Buddhist Thailand and Myanmar the rites of passage to adulthood and maturity are motherhood for women and ordination as a novice monk for men (Falk 2007: 7; Kawanami 2013: 51–52). In Thailand and Myanmar every boy spends a short time in the monkhood and through this act of earthly denial he transfers merit (good karma) to his parents and lives up to the male ideal (Kawanami 2013: 51; Falk 2007). On the other hand, women are denied ordination into the monkhood and fulfil their ideal roles through motherhood (Falk 2007; Kawanami 2013). Since Thai society divides human beings into monks and laypeople, women who are part of the laity are inferior in rank and required to be very much involved in the secular world as managers of the family's finances. One way to accumulate good karma for a happy rebirth is by feeding the monks and looking after Buddhist temples and the *sangha* (Buddhist monkhood). Thus, due to the importance of the monkhood in the quest for salvation, Buddhist monks in Thailand have the highest status (higher than the Thai king, for example), and as such are entitled to privileges such as free education, free medical care and free or reduced fares for buses and trains (Falk 2007: 37).

Although women cannot be monks, there are women who renounce the world and become ascetics either temporarily (known as *chii phraams*) or permanently (known *as mae chiis*) (Falk 2007: 16). Anthropologist Monica Falk argues that "the Thai sangha's persistence of not opening their doors to women keeps female ascetics in an inferior religious status" (Falk 2007: 7), maintaining women's position in the lay domain (Falk 2007: 28). Instead they become "ambiguous women" – neither lay (since they are not wives and mothers), nor religious (Falk 2007). From the perspective of the *sangha, mae chiis* are merely lay women despite the fact that they have renounced the world and live in temples (Falk 2007: 29). While monks have the highest status and are endowed with privileges, these are not extended to women ascetics such as *mae chiis,* who are still considered part of the laity (Falk 2007: 37). *Mae chiis'* low status also stems from the perception that they have neglected to fulfil their gendered duty of looking after aged parents and siblings (Falk 2007: 37). While "the Buddhist temples used to have the most central position in Thai villages, and the monks were educators, sponsors of co-operative work activities, personal and social counsellors and ethical mentors", *mae chiis* had an ambiguous position that renders them invisible and alienated from society (Falk 2007: 39–41). That monks are gendered male is evident by the fact that *kathoey* (or transgender women) are not allowed to be monks (Falk 2007: 45).

A similar pattern can be found in Myanmar. Burmese women are prohibited from becoming monks (Kawanami 2013: 235). While men's renunciation from worldly pursuits to join the monkhood is common and is considered prestigious, women who do the same and enter nunneries are "disparaged" by society primarily because the decision transgresses norms of femininity (Kawanami 2013: 51–52). Parents vehemently oppose a daughter's decision to enter the nunnery not only because they are afraid of condemning their offspring to a life of ridicule and mockery, but because the decision implies that their child is rejecting her filial obligation to look after them in their old age (Kawanami 2013: 77). Hence, kinship ties and women's assigned roles in them keep them attached to the material world. Because nuns' attempts to establish nunneries embroil them in the mundane responsibility of owning and managing monastic property, another worldly occupation, they cannot truly renounce the world in the same way that men can (Kawanami 2013). The fact that there are as many as 50,000 Buddhist nuns in Myanmar illustrates that, despite these hindrances, women are attracted to this life because it gives them the opportunity not just for higher education, a teaching vocation and leadership, but also because for them it is the best way to achieve a meritorious life and a happy rebirth (Kawamani 2013: 233).

In Indonesia, Bianca J. Smith argues that "it is possible for a Muslim woman to inherit and acquire spiritual power, but it must be qualified by male Muslim leaders, and in order to maintain her authority she and those around her must constantly negotiate with the hegemonic male-dominated religious and cultural order" (Smith 2014: 83). Since women's identity is based on their roles and position in the kinship group, it is also possible for a male spiritual leader to transfer spiritual power to his wife, sisters and daughters, who are perceived as "embodiments of his power" (Smith 2014: 86). *Kyai* (or *ulama*) are Muslim leaders and scholars who are heads of the *pesantren* (traditional Javanese Islamic boarding schools). The respect given to a *kyai* is also bestowed on his wife and family members (Smith and Woodward 2014: 1–19). Thus, much like the way women access political power through their family connections (see Section 6), women can emerge in special cases as leaders of the *pesantren* or *tarekat* (in the Sufi order) through their links with male spiritual leaders.

Although women cannot be religious leaders, they are allowed to be spirit mediums. In Myanmar and Vietnam they enjoy prestige and social power even though they experience less prestige than male spirit mediums (Harriden 2012: 33; Endres 2011: 136–37). Muslim women in urban Malaysia have also been proactive in the teaching and practice of religious education in mosques, homes and the workplace, and at religious revivalist organizations (Frisk 2009: 185). In this way, Malaysian Muslim women have been able to claim the religious authority to perform rituals in homes independent of men and have therefore shown some agency in fashioning themselves as *mukmin* or "pious subjects" (Frisk 2009: 4, 23, 184–87).

3.3 Critiquing the Religious Roots of Oppression

One of the main tasks of feminists in the region has been to theorize the religious roots of women's oppression. For some this means reinterpreting religious texts using a feminist lens; for others it means changing some of the religious role models for women; and for yet others it means lobbying for women's religious leadership. Filipino Catholic nuns in the Philippines have focused their energies on dismantling the suffering Virgin Mary (Mater Dolorosa) as the ideal woman and replacing her with the woman as apostle of Jesus Christ (Roces 2012). Feminists have joined global movements to reread and reinterpret the Bible (in Christian feminist theology) and the Qur'an and *sunna* (practices of the Prophet that include the traditions/narrations of the *hadith*) (in Islamic feminism) using a gendered woman-friendly lens (Roces 2012; Afrianty 2015: 29; Basarudin 2016). Sisters in Islam (SIS), for example, is an NGO consisting of Malay Muslim professional women based in Kuala Lumpur and dedicated to "promoting an understanding of Islam that recognizes the principles of justice, equality, freedom, and dignity within a democratic nation state" (quoted in Basarudin 2016: 4). What is radical about this group is that SIS "are claiming the right to interpret the Qu'ran by virtue of a direct relationship with God" (Basarudin 2016: 5) The organization is proactive in the field of jurisprudence (*fiqh*) or the body of law based on human reason used to understand the *sharia* (especially since many members are lawyers). SIS's argument is that since *fiqh* "cannot be separated from the historical and cultural processes that produce exegetes and jurists," then, "these conceptions, which are a product of human agency, are amenable to change according to contemporary realities" (Basarudin 2016: 5). SIS's advocacy is expressed publicly through publications on the impact of polygamy on women's lives, information booklets on domestic violence and gender equality and through contesting what it perceives to be outdated *sharia* criminal offences such as the moral policing of women (Basarudin 2016). Similarly, in Indonesia, "Islamic Feminism can be defined as a feminist discourse and practice articulated within an 'Islamic paradigm'" (Badran 2002: 1). According to Dina Afrianty, "Islamic feminism believes that the struggle for equality within Islam should be based on rereading and reinterpreting the Qur'an and *hadith* in order to produce feminist interpretations of the *sharia*. It seeks justice, equality and women's rights directly from the Qur'an" (Afrianty 2015: 29). Likewise, Rachel Rinaldo's study of Islam and feminism in Indonesia suggests that members of Rahima, a Muslim women's rights NGO, and Fatayat (Nahdlatul Ulama), the women's wing of Indonesia's largest Muslim organization, "demonstrate *pious critical agency* as they seek out Islamic justifications for gender equality, and draw on discourses of transnational feminism and Islamic reformism, as well as Indonesia's Islamic heritage, to argue for women's rights and religious reform" (Rinaldo 2013: 63).

Since men's status and privilege emerge from their presumed superiority in the spiritual realm, it is not surprising that feminist activists have focused also on addressing gender discrimination in the religious sphere, including advocating that religious organizations open positions of religious leadership to women.

There has been an effort to establish a *bhikkuni* (women's monastic) order in Thailand, with Thai professor Chatsumarn Kabilsingh (now Dhammananda Bhikkhuni) receiving ordination in the Theravada tradition abroad (Falk 2010: 118–19). Some Thai Buddhists criticize her for her audacity, but even without the *sangha*'s approval she has been able to start a *bhikkuni* community at her temple south of Bangkok (Falk 2010: 119–20). This community is still not recognized by the Thai monkhood but it has been able to get support from the transnational *bhikkuni* movement (Falk 2010: 121). Thus, given the strong resistance to the campaign for women to acquire religious leadership, feminists appeal to the international feminist movement for support and legitimization outside their home base (Falk 2010).

4 Authoritarian Regimes Fashion Hegemonic Gender Ideals: Indonesia and Vietnam

4.1 Introduction

Authoritarian regimes have also been very proactive in the project of social engineering in the area of gender relations and in proposing their own state-endorsed hegemonic ideals. These ideals are legitimized in state ideology (whether communist, socialist or conservative) and promoted through the establishment of national organizations and through the educational curriculum. Such regimes also propose their own versions of the ideal man and woman. Using the case studies of Indonesia under Suharto's New Order (1965–98) and Vietnam since 1989, this section examines the authoritarian state's influence and impact in defining, promoting and policing feminine ideals in particular, as part of its agenda for the modern nation. The absence of a democratic space makes it difficult for activists to critique dominant ideals or promote change but women's organizations have also tried to negotiate with authoritarian states, with some limited success. Authoritarian regimes have also had the opportunity to produce and promote gender narratives. In these discourses, gender constructs have been fashioned to buttress state policies for development or in response to the nation in crises such as war (for example, in Vietnam). Given that the political leadership of these countries has been and continues to be in the hands of men, the result is that these gender ideals have been biased in favour of men despite official rhetoric produced about gender equality in socialist regimes such as in Vietnam.

Indonesia's New Order ideology (1965–98) was premised on the belief that "Indonesian society should rest on the 'family principle' (*asas keluarga*) and on normative sex/gender roles where the head of the household was male" (Andaya 2018: 39). Julia Suryakusuma has coined the term "state ibuism" (since *ibu* means "mother") to refer to the state's ideology endorsing and propagating the image of women as mothers, educators of children and guardians of the family (Suryakusuma 1996). The Dharma Wanita (an organization of civil servants' wives) and the Family Welfare Association (PKK) have helped propagate these state constructions of the feminine as mere "appendages" of men who must donate to the state their unpaid labor in being housewives and supporting their husbands (Andaya 2018: 19; Suryakusuma 1996). For example, the PKK was responsible for marshaling the involvement of women in maternal and child health programs, which included vaccination of infants, and disseminating knowledge on modern health and nutrition practices (Robinson 2008: 75). Thus, during the New Order period, the role of wife and mother was promoted as the basis for female citizenship (Robinson 2018). The regime propagated this ideal through the celebration of national days such as Mothers' Day, commemorating the 1928 Indonesian Women's Congress, and Kartini Day, which included healthy-baby competitions, events that endorsed the state's view of good motherhood, and promotion of the wearing of the *sarong kebaya*, which conflated women as bearers and wearers of national "tradition".

Family planning programs targeted wives, proposing an ideal femininity in posters and television advertisements "as the mother of the well-spaced, small family, who is calm and serene, and blessed with a curvaceous body, in contrast to her harassed and scrawny sister, with her tribe of tiny children clutching at her knees" (Robinson 2008: 78). On the other hand, President Suharto was touted as the "father of development" and civil servants used the familial form of address (*bapak* for "father") to their usually male superiors (Robinson 2008: 70). According to the Marriage Law of 1974, men were heads of households and women were the housekeepers (Robinson 2008: 71). In public life women were known by their husbands' names (Robinson 2008: 76). The New Order hegemonic masculinity had a "violent and militaristic form" symbolized by state-sponsored violence such as sexual violation and murder of labor activists and the rape and murder of women in East Timor (Robinson 2008: 70).

In Vietnam, the state's construction of gender has experienced seismic shifts. During the war with the United States of America, socialist ideologies and wartime policies led to what Esta Ungar has described as a "de-gendering" of the economic and political sphere up until 1973/75 (Ungar 1994). In this period, both men and women were soldiers and many women entered traditional male occupations, doing agricultural work while men were fighting the war. Women became leaders of cooperatives and carried food and munitions to the frontlines and, as nurses, couriers, guides and propagandists, composed "the long-haired army" (Fahey 1998: 235). As members of the proletarian workforce their children were looked after in nationwide crèches (Fahey 1998: 235). This de-gendering of the populace was manifested in the visual art of propaganda posters, where both sexes were depicted with very few gender markers as they wore similar dress (black pajamas) and women did not wear cosmetics (Lowe 1994). The state trumpeted the ideal of "heroic femininity," where women were expected to give up their husbands and sons for the war effort, live chastely through the war and "defend the rear" by managing farms and homes, but also through care work such as nursing wounded soldiers (Pettus 2003: 42–52). The Communists proposed the removal of the Confucian-mandated "three obediences," which required women to obey their fathers, husbands and sons, but did not dismantle women's traditional inferior status to men (Pettus 2003: 8–9). While the Communist Party motivated women to take on new leadership roles in farming and industry, they were still expected to fulfill traditional household and caring roles in the family – duties that were still elevated as more important than public activities or employment (Pettus 2003: 39; Werner 2009: 3). These contradictory discourses that privileged women's location and roles in families as paramount continued even after the reforms of the Renovation Era or post-1989 (Werner 2009: 3).

The Vietnam Women's Union (VWU) disseminated official ideals about women to the populace through its propaganda journal and activities such as training sessions, contests, pageants and women's clubs (Pettus 2003: 17–18). Established in 1930, the VWU is a mass organization meant to advance the rights and represent the interests of women, which boasted a membership of over 15 million in 10,472 local units as of 2012 (Hoang 2020). It implements the state's policies on women's issues (Schuler et al. 2006: 384). The state-sanctioned VWU is the only "women's movement" in Vietnam. Since it is part of the state itself it does not have much room to resist state objectives, though it might have some wiggle room in promoting gender equality through its links with international NGOs (Chiricosta 2010: 139). The VWU succeeded in pushing for the passage of the Law on Gender Equality signed in 2006. This law has aimed to improve women's participation in the economic, political and social fields (Chiricosta 2010: 140).

From the late 1980s, there have been several contradictory images of the Vietnamese woman circulating in official discourse, resulting from differences in class, locality (rural versus urban) and whether she worked as a peasant or as a professional woman (Ungar 1994: 61–72). Beauty contests have been reintro-duced to Vietnam since 1989 (Fahey 1998: 228), with a Miss Ao Zai (Vietnamese national dress for women) contest restoring the traditional confla-tion of "woman as bearer and wearer of national tradition." In the VWU contest for "Building the Civilized and Happy Family" in Ba Dinh District in 1994, women contestants wore the Vietnamese *ao dai*, while male participants wore the Western suit (Pettus 2003: 94). Thus, the post-renovation period (since 1989) has introduced a re-gendering of Vietnam, with media images of the beautiful good wife and mother who keeps a clean house (using a new washing machine) attired in national dress making a comeback alongside ideals of the professional woman and the working peasant (Fahey 1998: 244; Ungar 1994; 2000). In contrast to the period of de-gendering when both men and women wore similar attire, the VWU from 1973 has promoted the wearing of skirts instead of "drab-coloured trousers" (Pettus 2003: 57).

From the 1990s onwards, the "new Vietnamese woman" – the state's official female ideal – has been the Vietnamese middle-class "enlightened housewife" and caring mother whose major role is to produce a happy, healthy and wealthy family, epitomized by the VWU campaign for the "Happy and Civilized Family" (Pettus 2003: 22; Leshkowich 2014: 12). The state also promoted its definition of the "Cultured Family," designed to reduce population growth (encouraging two children per family) and modernize and develop the economy (Drummond 2004: 158–78). In these attempts at socially engineering gender, women "are cast as 'traditional' nurturers, educators, regulators of harmony; there is in public discussion little emphasis on women as producers only as reproducers" (Drummond 2004: 167). As the state shifted its endeavors to strengthening the household and the family, the VWU focused its campaigns on women's domestic identities and their image as moral managers of the household, providing women with knowledge of birth control, nutrition, modern hygiene and parenting, for example (Pettus 2003: 87 and 90).

The new feminine ideal touted by the state is the "competent and caring middle-class housewife – a domestically committed woman who is enlightened by science, educated about tradition and untainted by the market's immoralities" (Pettus 2003: 109). The list of issues associated with "immoralities" includes drug addiction, the greed of business managers, gambling and marital infidelity (Pettus 2003: 104). Hence, the Vietnamese state wanted women to be moral guardians, much like in pre-revolutionary days. Jayne Werner argues that these new femininities "tended to be much more family-oriented, virtuous, and consumer-oriented than in the past" (Werner 2009: 4), while Lan Ah Hoang points out that the emphasis in the 1980s and 1990s was on household economics and childcare duties (Hoang 2020). Thus, we see that the Vietnamese state has also used constructions of gender "as a form of state power" and has manipulated gender ideals to suit priorities in state policies (Werner and Bélanger 2002: 23). These state discourses on the feminine have been more about fostering social stability and fulfilling economic goals (i.e., promoting the rising middle class) than achieving gender equality in the family and household (Werner 2009: 12).

It is, however, possible for individual citizens to resist the strong arm of authoritarian states in individual ways, such as through intimate relationships like marital relations. These are places where it is possible for individuals to exercise everyday forms of resistance to state laws that govern gender discourses, whether to promote gender equality or to undermine it. In Indonesia, the Marriage Law of 1974, enacted to give men and women equal rights to divorce, promotes monogamy giving strict conditions for men who want to take more than one wife (Blackburn 2004: 132–33; Platt 2017: 5; O'Shaughnessy 2009). It does, however, allow polygamy (Nurmila 2009: 153). But, in practice, religious courts and the social community are able to exert more influence than state law. In Sasak society (Lombok, Indonesia), the question of whether a couple is considered divorced or still married "remains a community-based affair" (Platt 2017: 5). Maria Platt argues that most couples experience a "marriage continuum" where "unions tend to be fluid in nature with people moving in and out of marriage, sometimes several times over the course of their lives" (Platt 2017: 5). Thus, in western Lombok, couples do not generally take advantage of the Marriage Law of 1974, and the perception of the local community appears to have more clout than whether the couple registered a divorce or marriage in the civil or religious court (Platt 2017).

Taking a different angle, Nina Nurmila's ethnography on the practice of polygamy in everyday life in contemporary Indonesia reveals how polygamous husbands disobey the law. The wives in polygamous marriages often suffer from husbands' lack of economic and social support despite the organized and pedantic use of rosters meant to divide husbands' time equally among all co-wives and children (Nurmila 2009: 20 and 146–254). Anthropological work on marriage, polygamy and gender reveal the many ways the state and even religious courts are not able to police these practices, while underscoring and documenting the myriad ways that the community and the kinship group are able to exercise everyday power on marital and intimate relationships in local communities.

The authoritarian states of Indonesia and Vietnam have been proactive in promoting their gender ideals in the name of "modernity" and the "national interest." These are not the only countries in Southeast Asia whose governments have been guilty of fashioning the feminine and the masculine. The People's Action Party (PAP) government of Singapore, which scholar Jasmine Chan described as a "patriarchal state" in the 1980s, reached its zenith in the 1980s, when Prime Minister Lee Kuan Yew's National Day Rally speech in 1983 provoked the Great Marriage Debate (Chan 2000: 47). This speech introduced a crisis discourse that argued that since eugenics was responsible for passing on intelligence to one's offspring, Singapore's competitive edge was at stake because single college-educated women were marrying later and having fewer children. The solution presented for this crisis had the effect of relocating women back into the home (with incentives for having more children), with university quotas introduced to favor men over women (Chan 2000: 47). The women's movement has succeeded in modifying some of the effects of these policies. For example, in 2005 the government acknowledged that men and women are equal as "heads of households" (Lyons 2010: 84). But the PAP's motivations were much like that of the authoritarian states of Vietnam and Indonesia; the state was willing to launch strict policies to alter gender ideals that had the potential to fundamentally alter the status of men and women. In all these cases, the state's gender ideals privileged heterosexual men over women, perhaps reflecting the fact that the leadership positions in these authoritarian regimes were mostly held by men.

4.2 The Impact of Social and Economic Transformations on State-Sanctioned Discourses

Economic and social forces have also had a massive role in undermining official discourses of gender roles. At the same time that the Suharto regime promoted motherhood and domesticity, it also wanted women to enter the workforce in order to promote development (Van Wichelen 2010; Robinson 2008). The regime's industrialization and manufacturing strategies had the effect of feminizing the workforce, as women began to make up 80 percent of the workforce in the textiles, clothing and footwear industries (which by the late 1990s contributed to 55 percent of Indonesia's exports; Robinson 2008: 90). In the period from 1974 to 1984, women were also entering the civil service, represented in 41 percent of middle-rank levels (Robinson 2008: 95).[3] These realities could be somewhat reconciled with the state-sanctioned gender discourse valorizing women's roles as wives and mothers by depicting women's work as being just "on the side" (*sampingan*), with their income as merely supplementary or "helping" (*bantu-bantu*) their husbands' (Robinson 2008: 91). Yet with the growing number of women in their teens and twenties eventually making up the majority of the manufacturing workforce (Robinson 2008: 96), it became obvious that everyday realities did not dovetail with the official discourse. If we fast-forward to the post-Suharto era, young women and their parents now generally expect women to have careers after marriage, not least because a career is interpreted as an important return on the "investment" into the daughter's education (Smith-Hefner 2018; 2019). These shifts

---

[3] There is some evidence that democratization in post-Suharto Indonesia worsened the career prospects of women in the civil service (Pierskalla et al. 2021).

from viewing women as "housewives" to seeing them as "career-women" did not happen overnight and arguably have their roots in the economic changes promoted by the Suharto regime, despite that regime heavily touting its hegemonic ideal that women should be housewives. Anthropologist Nancy Smith-Hefner has also demonstrated that despite the conservative Islamic version of Javanese masculinity that requires the father and husband to be the breadwinner, competing masculinities have now appeared where prospective grooms dream of a romantic companionate marriage where wives work as part of the couple's shared dream of achieving a middle-class lifestyle (Smith-Hefner 2018; 2019).

The Vietnamese state's essentializing of women as mothers and carers while de-emphasizing their professional achievements likewise contradicts the growing number of independent career women, some of whom employ domestic workers, who have also appeared as a consequence of the state's policies of opening up the market economy (Hoang 2020). Vietnamese women dominate the marketplace and as clothing merchants, for example, often earn more money than their husbands (Leskowich 2014), and many have professional careers in the city (Earl 2014). According to Catherine Earl, educated migrants move to Ho Chi Minh City, where they have the opportunity to launch professional careers (Earl 2014: 13). The feminization of this migration pattern has been a trend since the Renovation Era, where there are opportunities for jobs in the non-state sector and where two-thirds of those employed in businesses supported by foreign investment and nearly half of the private sector are women (Earl 2014: 13–14). A lot of single women go to the city to further their education or to find jobs as housekeepers, salesgirls, hostesses, hairdressers, manicurists, masseusses and waitresses (Peters 2016: 36). Some of these career women, who are also mothers, have even received "prizes" from the Vietnam Womens' Union for being "accomplished in schoolwork, adept at housework" – awards that endorse hegemonic state ideals and highlight the contradictions between representations and realities. The informants in Lan Anh Hoang's study demonstrate their blasé attitude toward these awards by mocking their modest financial prizes (500,000 dong or US$22), the bureaucratic paperwork associated with the nomination process and the way they are simply handed out methodically to women when it is "their turn to win" (Hoang 2020). The irony of it all is that many women receive these awards and are able to have careers because they have domestic servants to help them with domestic duties (the "adept at housework" part of the criteria) and caring duties (helping their children with their homework) (Hoang 2020: 297–98). This goes to show that middle-class and elite women's careers are built on the domestic labor of lower-class women. These examples from Vietnam reveal that it is very possible to resist an authoritarian state and mock its ideals but they also imply that other women may be paying the price for this rebellion.

5 Desire and Sexualities

5.1 Introduction

In Southeast Asia, hegemonic discourses on gender and sexuality are exceedingly complex and are imbricated not only with concepts of family, community and nation, but also with morality, and the policing of desire. This section examines hegemonic discourses on desire and sexuality, as well as subordinated sexualities, in Indonesia, Thailand and the Philippines. It argues that Southeast Asian hegemonic discourses expect men to be naturally lustful and women to be chaste beings devoid of desire. These premises set the conceptual parameters around beliefs about sexuality, which are in turn linked to gender ideals, so that women who do not conform to the norm are demonized, ostracized or judged to have been a victim of black magic. The result is that Southeast Asian societies subject most women to sexual surveillance aimed at policing their desires. In some Southeast Asian states sex is only sanctioned with the institution of heterosexual marriage. These states also produce hegemonic discourses that connect sexualities with morality and national identities. In this paradigm, those who transgress these hegemonic discourses are placed outside the nation, such that they are un-Thai or un-Cambodian, for example, or are guilty of treason. It is extremely difficult for many Southeast Asians to break from the hegemonic gender-sexual constructs, not only because these have become their only social reality, but because of the heavy social and state surveillance that they confront daily. Hence, I also contend that it is often migrants who are able to imagine an alternative view of gender and desire that challenges the norms in the homeland.

5.2 Virile Men and Chaste Women

The dominant Filipino cultural belief does not sanction a women's right to sexuality (Estrada-Claudio 2002: 20). Sylvia Estrada-Claudio notes that while sexual experience for men is part of becoming male, the suppression of sexuality is an intrinsic part of the cultural construction of being female, with Narzalina Lim, former undersecretary of the Department of Tourism, even claiming that females are conditioned to be anti-sexual (Estrada-Claudio, quoted in Torres 2002: 138; Lim, quoted in Garcellano et al. 1992: 26). In this hegemonic Filipino cultural discourse, women cannot be agents capable of desire but are instead beautiful objects of desire, while men are "naturally" lustful (Estrada-Claudio, quoted in Torres 2002: 9). Filipino hegemonic masculinity, still an under-researched field and still untheorized, is connected to a man's fertility, virility and capacity to attract women, his skills as provider and his ability to attract followers or allies (Pingol 2001; McKay 2007; McKay and Lucero-Prisno III 2012). Many Filipino men have mistresses, a practice tolerated by society. In fact, one can argue that a man with a mistress enjoys considerable status since virility and power are linked. Politicians such as President Ferdinand Marcos, a well-known womanizer, and President Joseph Estrada, a movie star with several mistresses, have received popular support unharmed by the sex scandals in their lives. It is common for rich men to have mistresses since they are financially able to lavish them with gifts. Filipino society's tolerance for this *querida* system (meaning "beloved" in Spanish, a euphemism for a mistress) made it possible for a book entitled *Etiquette for Mistresses* to become a bestseller in the 1990s and a blockbuster movie in 2015. However, there are limits. The public chastises those who use ill-gotten wealth to support the lifestyle of their mistresses or if they let the "other woman" exercise unofficial power. The events leading to the impeachment trial of Estrada included reportage on the extravagant mansions he built for his girlfriends, while Rosemarie Arenas, the alleged mistress of President Fidel Ramos, was criticized heavily for meddling in politics

But while men's infidelity is generally tacitly accepted by society, with the excuse that it is part of their nature to be lustful, the female ideal is to be devoid of sexual desire. Even so, women gain status from being objects (rather than agents) of desire. Women must be beautiful and attractive. A contemporary study conducted in 2001–02 in two rural communities in the Philippines revealed that, while personality was an important factor when women assessed a potential male suitor, for men "Beauty and comeliness underlie one's choice of a wife" (Torres 2002: 41). Although virility is linked to male power, beauty is linked to female power (Roces 1998: ch. 5). Society places pressure on every female, single or married, to be beautiful (according to the Filipino cultural measure of beauty); if a husband has mistresses, the wife is often blamed for not being beautiful enough.

By the same token, beauty contests are obsessively popular in many countries of Southeast Asia (with rare exceptions such as Malaysia, where they are largely banned) and are ubiquitous even among diasporic communities. Beauty titles, no matter how humble (such as being a muse of a basketball team, or Little Miss Philippines-Australia), bestow enormous cultural capital on the women who hold them. People view beauty queens as role models and ideal women not because they exude sexuality but precisely because they embody the hegemonic gender ideal, which connects female beauty with a woman's virtue. The point is that beauty (*maganda*) in the Philippine cultural and linguistic context refers not just to physical beauty but to conduct that is socially pleasing. The Tagalog word *maganda* does not simply mean beautiful; it is connected with what society considers good or virtuous. For example, the government appointed Gemma Cruz, the first Filipina to win the Miss International beauty contest, director of the National Museum (Araneta 2018) shortly after her coronation, and politicians often invite beauty title-holders to run for political office (Roces 1998). In Indonesia, policewomen are expected to be beautiful since "the phenomenon of the pretty policewoman" sends the message that she is moral, incorruptible and just (Davies 2018: 69–88; 2015b).

The idealization of women as objects of desire who are unable to perform desire also explains the connection between virginity and women's honor and value. The acceptable narrative is that women must be virginal daughters before they marry and chaste wives afterwards. Sex is sinful except in the context of marriage; because ideal women are incapable of lust, a wife's submission to her husband's demands for sex is explained in the context of wifely duty.

This oppositional conceptual divide that I have described in the Philippine situation, where men are naturally lustful and women are denied sexual rights, applies to practically the entire region of Southeast Asia. Evelyn Blackwood (2007: 25; 2010: 141), Linda Rae Bennett (2005: 31) and Megan Sinnott (2004: 115–18), writing respectively on West Sumatra, Lombok and Thailand, all argue that women are supposed to be lacking in sexual desire or "devoid of sexual needs" (Sinnott 2004: 115) except that they need to have sex in order to bear children (Bennett 2005: 31). In Cambodia and Thailand, it is not uncommon for a young man to lose his virginity with a prostitute (Cook 1998: 260; Jacobsen 2008: 191), but all women are expected to remain virgins until they marry. While Thai cultural beliefs assume that prostitutes are essential because men's sexual needs are "natural and in need of fulfillment," "discourses of sex used in Thai society consistently negate women as sexual agents" (Sinnott 2004: 116).

In an excellent and rare study of single women and sexuality in the region, Linda Rae Bennett distinguishes between female purity and male promiscuity in Mataram in Lombok, Indonesia. According to her, both *adat* ("traditional custom") and Islam "are generally synthesized in a manner that denies women their right to sexual autonomy, accords women greater responsibility for upholding sexual morality, and protects men's relative sexual freedom" (Bennett 2005: 23). On the other hand, "sex with female prostitutes was common for unmarried men and is tacitly accepted as normative behaviour" (Bennett 2005: 26). Male desire is considered "wild, unrestrained and inherently dangerous" so that "aggressive male sexuality is juxtaposed with the sanctity of female chastity" (Bennett 2005: 96). Signs of women's sexual autonomy are either dismissed as signs of the supernatural, or reinterpreted in a way that casts women to be victims or as martyrs. A good illustration of this is the story of Uma, a woman from Lombok who abandoned her fiancé to follow a man she met in a bar one night all the way to his hometown in Bali. Her village community did not interpret her impulsive behavior as a product of earthly lust; instead she was rumoured to be a victim of love magic (*pelet*) (Bennett 2005: 84–104).

The Thai view is that female prostitutes are really dutiful daughters earning a living under extreme conditions of poverty in order to send money to the family (Cook 1998). Feminist activists in the Philippines represent prostitutes as "victims" who are "bought" or "sold," not as agents who are "selling sex" (Roces 2012: 60). The contemporary Philippine media represents mistresses as kept women – in other words, as agreeing to a sexual relationship because the man is providing for them, or possibly their family, not because they enjoy having sex with him. In Java, people believe that "a woman will not agree to have extramarital sexual relations with a man unless there is some palpable benefit to be gained from it, preferably of an economic sort" (Brenner 1998: 152), and wives are often willing to tolerate infidelity but are more concerned that their husband's unfaithfulness may result in a financial drain away from their legitimate family (Brenner 1998: 152–57). All these representations deny women's sexual agency.

Throughout Southeast Asia, dominant social norms expect a young unmarried maiden to be beautiful enough to attract a man and make him want to marry her – but after she succeeds in getting him to notice her, she is required to protect her virginity at all costs. This is an enormous challenge since to fulfil masculine sexual ideals the suitor is often expected to attempt to seduce her. Women have to come up with their own strategies to protect their virginity. Women in Lombok, Mataram must exude an almost impossible-to-achieve look of what Bennett terms "sensual modesty" (Bennett 2005: 54). In recent years, they have done so by veiling and presenting themselves as pious Muslims (Bennett 2005: 49–56). Since the practice of courtship makes a woman vulnerable to seduction, the kinship group is tasked with the responsibility for protecting her purity. Sexual transgressions – that is, infidelity, adultery or pre-marital sex – are not simply viewed as one individual's sin. The entire family becomes tainted in what Sharyn Graham Davies and Linda Rae Bennett have eloquently called "kinships of shame" (Davies and Bennett 2015: 13; Davies 2015: 33). Among the Bugis in Sulawesi, if an unmarried woman becomes pregnant, it is not interpreted as being solely her fault because it is assumed that her family should have been protecting her; thus, the whole family loses status and is tainted with the disgrace (Davies 2007: 35). Since the family's honor is at stake, family members guard women tightly, subjecting them to "vigilant surveillance" and prohibiting them from traveling alone to make sure they have an unblemished reputation (Bennett 2005; Davies 2015; 2007: 35–36). Such policing of women is also justified by the need to protect them from love magic, which could result in awakening their sexual urges (Bennett 2005).

The antithesis of the virginal maiden and the chaste wife is the widow or the divorcee. The prevailing discourse in Indonesia is that widows and divorcees (called *janda* in Indonesian) are "promiscuous women" since they are no longer attached to a man (and therefore not subject to moral policing), and, unlike young unmarried maidens, already have carnal knowledge. The term *janda* is pejorative, suggesting a sexually experienced but deprived woman who is lonely, weak and desperate for a new man in her life (Mahey et al. 2016: 47–67). *Janda* are both pitied and desired but are also stigmatized as of low status. They are always the subject of salacious gossip; others marginalize them from certain social activities expected of married women (Mahey et al. 2016: 47–67). The *janda*'s subject position locates them outside the acceptable norm of "married woman." Unlike married women who are considered to be chaste, *janda* are judged to be disgraced and immoral (Parker et al. 2016: 27–46). The figure of the *janda* suggests women's sexual autonomy and therefore is perceived to be dangerous and abnormal.

Since the ideal woman is incapable of sexual desire, the most effective way to destroy a woman's reputation is to suggest that she is hypersexual or to associate her with deviant sexual behaviour. For example, during the 1965–66 coup d'état that toppled President Sukarno of Indonesia, when the army and its allies massacred a million communists, the military circulated rumors that members of GERWANI (Gerakan Wanita Indonesia or the Indonesian Women's Movement) had castrated the kidnapped generals and afterwards danced naked in the moonlight (Wieringa 2002). Saskia Wieringa, whose important study of GERWANI first brought the issues of sexual politics in Indonesia to light, argues that Suharto was able to legitimize the violence targeted at the Indonesian Communist Party (PKI) by spreading these accusations of sexual debauchery purportedly committed by members of GERWANI, which was connected to the PKI (Wieringa 2002: 1). Prior to the fall of Sukarno, GERWANI had a mass following (1.5 million in 1963) (Blackburn 2010: 26; 2004: 178) but the strategy of linking women's political activity with sexual depravity succeeded in destroying its membership base, which to this day has not been rebuilt (Wieringa 2002: 1).

Similar phenomena are found elsewhere in the region. Before 2012, when the Tatmadaw (Burmese army) wanted to discredit their rival Aung San Suu Kyi (the daughter of nationalist hero Aung San), they said she was driven by lust (Peletz 2012: 901). President Rodrigo Duterte of the Philippines hoped to humiliate his loudest critic Senator Leila de Lima and intimidate her into silence by threatening to disseminate an alleged tape of the senator having sex with her driver, with whom she was having an affair (Cepeda 2016). Senator de Lima was separated from her husband, so she was not technically committing adultery, but the very suggestion that a single woman was having sex with a man who was not her husband was supposed to expose her to be untrustworthy. It is not considered unusual or scandalous that Duterte himself confided that he had had many girlfriends, and it is common knowledge that many politicians keep mistresses. However, people tend to view it as reprehensible if a woman is having sex with a person who is not her spouse, and it is even more "shameful" if it is with someone of a lower class/status than herself.

5.3 Subordinated Sexualities

I have described above the dominant discourses on gender and sexuality in Southeast Asia. Alternative sexualities do exist, of course, and in a plethora of varieties. The taboo on discussions about sexuality is the reason why it is difficult for people who are not heterosexual to "come out" publicly (Davies 2007: 50–52). In the Philippines, until the 1990s there was no public discussion of female sexuality outside debates about prostitution (Roces 2012). Since states in some countries deem non-heterosexual sexualities "illegal," I adopt the term "subordinated" sexualities (Smith-Hefner 2018: 85–106).

Since women are not supposed to feel sexual desire, Thais find it difficult to imagine the possibility of sex between two women (Sinnott 2004: 116). This does not mean that romantic pairings between women who love women do not exist. They do. However, for the most part, specific labels for such women who love women only began to appear in the closing decades of the twentieth century. In Thailand the terms "tom" to refer to masculine women (short for the English "tomboy") and "dee" to refer to the female partner of a tom appeared only in the late 1970s (Sinnott 2004: 2).

Women who dress and act like men (or transmen – or female-bodied transgender males) are called *calalai* (which literally means "false man"), "hunter" or "tomboy" in South Sulawesi, *tomboi* in Padang, West Sumatra, "butch" in Jakarta and "tom" in Thailand (Davies 2007; Blackwood 2010; Sinnott 2004). Their female partners are called "dees" in Thailand, *lines* or *cewek* in South Sulawesi (*cewek*, meaning "female" in colloquial Indonesian, is also the term for the feminine lesbians (*lesbi*) in the Indonesian archipelago) and "femme" in Padang, West Sumatra (Boellstorff 2005: 9; Davies 2007; Sinnott 2004; Blackwood 2010). These dees and femmes, however, typically identify as heterosexual women, not as a different gender. In day-to-day relationships, they perform normative female tasks such as domestic chores including cooking, cleaning and serving guests (Blackwood 2010). Yet, they also challenge female gender norms by taking the role of assertive sexual partner – a radical move that is not conceivable in societies that cannot imagine that women might have erotic feelings (Davies 2007: 58).

A male-bodied transgender female or transwoman is called a *calabai* in South Sulawesi and a *kathoey* (or "lady boy") in Thailand. In Indonesia, *waria* is the term used to refer to a male-bodied individual who acts like a woman. *Waria* (the term's origins come from *wanita-pria* or "woman-man") are not a third gender like the *bissu*; instead they are a male femininity (Boellstorff 2004: 159–95). According to Neil Garcia, in the Philippines the word *bakla* became "homo/sexualized as an identity" in the 1970s (Garcia 1996: 71). The *bakla* is "a male whose object of sexual desire is another male, but who, by virtue of this peculiarity of object choice, loses his maleness, and begins to turn into a female" (Garcia 1996: 54). Mark Johnson's excellent, pioneering work argues that the *bantut* in the southern Philippines define themselves as being like women and therefore as sexual partners assume the role of the female and are penetrated by men (Johnson 1997). This group developed its own language (called *swardspeak*) in the 1970s. Men who love men are much more visible than women who love women, because women's desire is considered taboo, and women are much more subject to kinship surveillance than their male counterparts. In the Philippines and Indonesia from at least the 1970s, *bakla* and *waria* tended to congregate in beauty parlors or salons, or in couture houses, which became unofficial gay spaces of work (Davies 2007: 61–81; Johnson 1997). Gay men have also been able to carve out public spaces for themselves, mostly bars or malls in urban centres such as Metro-Manila and Jakarta (Benedicto 2014; Boellstorff 2004). In the southern Philippines, they have succeeded in proposing their own definitions of beauty, which they channel from American styles and global beauty contests (Johnson 1997).

The consumer power of middle-class gay men has not gone unnoticed as the power of what is termed the "pink dollar" or the "purple *baht*" has fuelled the "queer boom" in Bangkok in the twenty-first century, increasing real queer spaces in the urban jungle such as bars, saunas, restaurants and discos (Weiss 2007: 165; Jackson 2011: 17–42; Wilson 2004: 120). In Singapore, the growth of a "gay consumer space that provided lifestyle options for local queers and gay tourists alike" made it possible for "representations of homosexuality to thrive" (Yue et al. 2017: 752–53). In contrast, toms have not been able to claim their own dedicated public space in Bangkok and have to make do with the usual female spaces such as restaurants and shopping areas (Wilson 2004: 120–21).

In South Sulawesi, the *calabai*–men relationships that Davies observed are predominantly contractual relationships. In these arrangements, the *calabai* invite their male lovers to cohabit and, in return, they agree to support their partners financially and give them an expensive gift when the contract ends (Davies 2007: 71–74). Their male partners do not consider themselves to be homosexuals. Garcia points out that it is not unusual for homosexual men in Manila to pay for sexual favours from "callboys." In Chiang Mai, Thailand, the men who accept money for sex with homosexual men are called "bar boys" because they work in gay bars (van Wijngaarden 1999: 193–318). While homosexual men in the Philippines and Thailand who pay for sex are gay, their "callboy" or "bar boy" partners do not consider themselves to be homosexuals (Garcia 1996: 92–96; van Wijngaarden 1999: 193–218; Johnson 1997).

Anthropologist Evelyn Blackwood points out that the Southeast Asian hegemonic ideal is that all men and women must marry in order to be considered adults and respectable citizens, and they must marry someone of the opposite sex (Blackwood 1999: 191; Boellstorff 2005: 103 and 117). In Sulawesi, Indonesia, not marrying jeopardizes the family's honor (Davies 2007: 39). This crucial rite of passage to adulthood, which Tom Boellstorff (2005) labels "the marriage imperative," pressures gays, *lesbis*, *tombois*, dees, toms, *waria*, *calalai* and *calabai* to live double lives as married men and women while also finding ways to express and live true to their underlying sexual orientations. In the public eye, they appear to be a heterosexual person married to the "correctly prescribed" gender, but at the same time they live a secret life involving romantic trysts with their same-sex lover. *Calalai* and *cewek* accept the fact that they could be together until parental pressure to marry becomes so great that they must part. This understanding of the inevitability of marriage motivates both partners to preserve their virginity by limiting their sexual encounters to hugging and kissing (Blackwood 2010: 140–42). The cultural axiom that women are not capable of sexual desire makes this arrangement possible (Blackwood 2010: 131; Sinnott 2004). The dee may marry a heterosexual man and may decide to carry on her sexual liaison with a tom. A *calalai* can also marry a *waria* (Davies 2007: 54). Or a gay man might marry a heterosexual woman and continue his sexual affair with another man in secret (Boellstorff 2005: 202).

According to Tom Boellstorff, in Indonesia, when a gay man turns to his lover in bed and tells him to marry a woman, he is not internalizing homophobia; instead, he is accepting the reality of the marriage imperative and its intimate connection with the kinship group (Boellstorff 2005: 202). These gay men want their partners to marry a woman because: "why would you want to hurt your parents by not marrying? How will you think of yourself as an adult, as complete?" (Boellstorff 2005: 202). Since divorce is allowed in Indonesia, one of the strategies deployed by *lesbi* women is to marry a man and then have a divorce (ideally after giving birth to a child so as to fulfil the gender expectations for women), and then continue to have romantic relationships with women (Blackwood 2010: 153–58; Davies 2007: 52–60; Boellstorff 2005: 111–14). Of course, once women are divorced, they risk experiencing the stigma of the *janda*.

The strategy of living a double life is only effective because transgressive sexuality (Blackwood 2010) escapes social ostracism, or social sanctions, if public appearance conforms to normative expectations (Jackson and Sullivan 1999: 4). Although the persons living double lives do not see themselves as bisexual (Boellstorff 2005: 206), the category of bisexual does exist in the semantics of Filipinos and Thais. According to Garcia, "the *silahis* is a male who looks every bit like a 'real man', may even be married and with a family," but "unlike *bakla* – the sexual object choice of whom is defined by some immanent, internalized identity, and not necessarily by the sexual act itself – the *silahis* is a genital male whose erotic life, is being centered around both genital females and males becomes perceived to be a function as much of his activities as of his gender selfhood" (Garcia 1996: 110). In Thailand, there are several Thai idioms for bisexual but the most common is *seua bai*, which literally means "a double-edged knife that can cut with both sides of the blade" and is a "conflation of the Thai word for 'tiger' (*seua*) and the first syllable of the borrowed term *bai*, from the English word 'bisexual'" (van Wijngaarden 1999: 198–99; Jackson 1995: 61). The terms *silahis/seua bai* are usually applied to males only, and to date (as of 2021) there is no word to indicate bisexual women. This can be partially explained by the hegemonic ideal that women are incapable of sexual desire, making it difficult for Southeast Asian heterosexuals to conceive of a woman who desires both men and women. The topic of bisexuality in Southeast Asia is still under-researched, perhaps because the emergence of the bisexual movement globally only happened around the end of the 1980s and early 1990s (Garcia 1996: 111).

5.4 Sexuality, Morality and the State

In Southeast Asia sexualities can be highly politicized and are inextricably linked to moralities – both personal and national. The political leaders of Singapore and Malaysia, for example, have all claimed that non-heteronormative sexualities are a Western import that threaten "Asian values" and therefore must be expunged in order to protect the Asian heteronormative family (Peletz 2006: 322–24). As recently as 2016 in Indonesia, state officials, politicians, the press, civil society groups and conservative leaders described LGBT Indonesians as "products of 'Western intervention'" and therefore as "foreign" and "politically threatening" (Wijaya 2020: 2–3). A conservative Islamic pro-family group called Family Love Alliance (Aliansi Cinta Keluarga) in the same year tried "to outlaw consensual same-sex relations and extramarital relationships on the grounds that they 'endangered' the nation's morality and values" (Wijaya 2020: 2–3). Scholar Hendri Yulius Wijaya eloquently captures the link between sexualities, citizenship and the nation in Indonesia when he says in his pioneering book on LGBT activism in Indonesia: "Through defining LGBT persons as an emerging threat to the nation-state's traditional values and identity, these conservative forces seek to enhance their public persona as the nation's moral guardian, demanding the exclusion of queer people from national identity and belonging" (Wijaya 2020: 151).

Homosexuality is illegal in Singapore, although in January 2021 Singapore's Apex Court heard three challenges aiming to dismiss the law that criminalises sex between men (Yahoo! News Editorial Team 2021). In Malaysia while technically the law does *not* criminalize sexual or gender *identities*, Section 377 of the Penal Code "penalises those found guilty of engaging in 'carnal intercourse against the order of nature', defined as anal or oral sex involving the penis" (hui 2019: 5). However, there is also the *musahaqah*, in the Syariah Criminal Offences (Federal Territories) Act of 1997 that prohibits "sexual relations between female persons" (hui 2019: 201). The latter received media coverage in 2018 when two women were publicly caned in front of a crowd of 100 people because they were found guilty under the Terengganu Syariah Criminal Offences (SCO) Enactment of "attempting to have lesbian sex in a car" (hui 2019: 198).

In Indonesia, meanwhile, heterosexual marriage is widely seen as being intrinsic to an individual's civic duty (Robinson 2008; Boellstorff 2005; Surkusuyama 1996; Blackwood 2010: 62). Hendri Yulius Wijaya and Sharyn Graham Davies argue that while Indonesia's transition to democracy in 1998 enabled lesbian and gay activists to assert rights claims and demand acceptance of their sexual diversity, at the same time, their more public presence triggered a homophobia that was not seen during the New Order (Wijaya and Davies 2019: 153). According to Saskia Wieringa, "the increased visibility of LGBT people did not lead to greater acceptance but rather turned public opinion against them" (Wieringa 2019: 128). Since the 1990s, Indonesian state officials and clerics have begun to oppose homosexuality publicly (Blackwood 2010: 61). In 1994, Abdurrahman Wahid, a Muslim cleric who later became president of Indonesia, declared that "lesbianism is deviant and should not be condoned," while a minister of women's affairs in that same year remarked that "lesbianism is not part of Indonesian culture or state ideology" (quoted in Blackwood 2010: 61). In public discourses from 2010 to the time of writing lesbian and gay activists have been "positioned as a threat to national security and in need of overt regulation" (Wijaya and Davies 2019: 165), requiring the nation "to be defended against threats to its integrity and morality, defined as attacks on the Pancasila and Islam" (Wieringa 2019: 127).

The Islamic Defenders' Front (Front Pembela Islam, FPI), a religious vigilante group, prevented the running of lesbian and gay activities and conferences in 2010 (Wijaya and Davies 2019: 160–62). By 2016 there were campaigns to ban LGBT organizations from Indonesian university campuses, supported by political parties such as the National Awakening Party (Partai Kebangkitan Bangsa, PKB), a moderate Muslim party. The chair of the People's Consultative Assembly (Majelis Permusyawaratan Rakyat, MPR), Zulkifli Hasan, expressed the view that homosexuality should be banned (Wieringa 2019: 122–23). In January 2021, two men accused of having sex each received seventy-seven lashes from a rattan cane. This was the third public flogging for homosexuality in Aceh since the province implemented *sharia* law in 2015 (Wieringa 2021). (In May 2017, gay men were also flogged in Aceh for alleged homosexual acts (Wijaya and Davies 2019: 161).)

The link between sexualities and morality is of course a gendered one. According to Sharyn Graham Davies, writing on Indonesia: "state morality is readable on the skin of (female) citizens" (Davies 2018: 83) State morality is literally imposed on Indonesian policewomen, who are not only required to be single and beautiful, but are subjected to a virginity test because: "A pious, pure pretty woman signifies a morally robust nation" (Davies 2018: 80). The Indonesian state therefore views the sexual conduct of government employees to be connected to the moral legitimacy of the regime (Suryakusuma 1996: 92–119). The Malaysian government demonizes LGBT persons as "traitors to the nation" (Teik 2014: 364). In Cambodia, LGBT persons are represented as threats to "traditional" Khmer culture, and imagined to be "deviant" "criminals," "gang members" and even "thieves" (Hoefinger et al. 2016: 321). In Thailand, state discourses on abortion – arguably the biggest taboo in the area of reproductive rights in this region – represent it not only as a sin according to the Buddhist religion but as un-Thai as well (Whittaker 2004).

The intricate connection between sexuality and state morality has implications for policies on reproductive health. Contraception is normally referred to in the state discourses in Southeast Asia as "family planning," implying that only married people who want to limit the number of children they have in the family should have access to it. In Indonesia, the state-sponsored family planning program is available for married women but illegal for those who are not married (Bennett 2005: 36). Single women, especially young maidens from the lower classes, find it terribly difficult to access contraception at all, since it is considered shameful for unmarried women to purchase items such as condoms (Bennett 2005: 36). Abortion is illegal in the Philippines, Myanmar and Indonesia unless it is to save a woman's life (though in Indonesia it is also permitted in certain circumstances such as rape) (Roces 2012: 184–99; Wieringa 2015: 33; Sheehy et al. 2015: 475). This means that those who seek to access it clandestinely risk losing their lives because the procedure would be performed outside the hospital system, making patients more vulnerable to infection that may result in death (Roces 2012: 184–99; Sheehy et al. 2015).

Finally, I give a unique example of how a state deliberately desexualizes its citizens. In Singapore the state attempts to manage sexualities by sanctioning only heterosexual sex, and only for the purposes of procreation (so, for example, no oral sex unless it is a prelude for vaginal sexual intercourse) (Leong 2012). The Media Development Authority (MDA) regulates erotic materials and censors "films that depict explicit or perverted sex, nude scenes that are exploitative or obscene" with the rationale that Singaporeans are conservative about sex, and that its role is to preserve these "Asian values" from Western decadence (Leong 2012). Lawrence W. T. Leong suggests that the state deliberately desexualizes Singaporeans because it suits its economic policies to view them as "laboring subjects" needed to keep Singapore economically competitive in a globalized world; in other words, the relationship the state has with gay people is predicated on how they can contribute to the economy (Leong 2012). The title of Meredith Weiss' article on the topic of employment discrimination experienced by gay people in Singapore captures this sentiment: "We Know Who You Are. We'll Employ You" (Weiss 2007). Weiss points out that the Singapore government "took steps to style itself as tolerant," but these measures are mainly driven by economic interests. A quote from a newspaper columnist says it all: "Remember, this is not about gay rights. This is about economic competitiveness." This sends the message that gays are welcome as talented professional workers and have the right to earn a living, as long as they do not hold public parades (Weiss 2007: 165).

Discourses on sexualities are therefore very important and very visible in Southeast Asian politics where private sexual matters become imbued with discourses on nation, state and national identities. The state plays a big role in fashioning hegemonic constructions of gender and sexuality and justifies acts of policing the sexualities of individuals in the name of preserving imagined national identities. Activists who hope to alter these hegemonic ideals therefore face the challenge of dismantling the links between sexuality, morality and the state that have been so entrenched in Southeast Asia politics.

5.5 LGBT Activism

While activists have made advances in deconstructing dominant gender ideals and promoting awareness about gender issues to mainstream society, their advocacy is hindered by society's conceptual barriers, where certain issues remain "off-limits." For example, in Singapore, Lenore Lyons argues that this list of socially proscribed topics includes the rights of lesbians, religion, the role of *sharia* law and class-based social divisions (Lyons 2010: 85). Thus, activism by LGBT groups there became visible only in the mid-2000s. People Like Us (PLU), a gay advocacy group formed in 1993 though barred from having legal status, has been able to inspire new groups that cover the wide spectrum of LGBT persons in Singapore, such as Red Queen and Sayoni for lesbian and bisexual women, SgButterfly for transgendered people, PLUME for LGBT youth, Heartland.Sg for LGBT Buddhists, Safehaven for LGBT Christians, Sisters in Solidarity for transgender women, and Oogachaga, which provides counseling for all LGBTQ+ peoples (Leong 2012: 24–25; Weiss 2013: 165). This is remarkable given that so far (as of 2021) no LGBT or gay rights organization has been successful in registering under the Societies Act in Singapore because homosexuality is illegal (Lyons 2010: fn. 87; Leong 2012: 24; Weiss 2013: 165).

These constraints force activists to deploy creative strategies to promote advocacy for LGBT rights. In 2008, the Singapore government made it possible for the public to demonstrate at the Speaker's Corner within Hong Lim Park without having to obtain a police permit. Members of Singapore's LGBT communities used this opportunity to celebrate diversity through an event called the Pink Dot – promoted not as a protest but as celebrating the freedom of all Singaporeans to choose whom to love (Philipps 2014: 50). The celebration from 2011 represented itself as a "family event," "to emphasize the diversity of Singaporean families and the importance of kinship." This representation deliberately desexualized Pink Dot and, combined with a lack of a specific LGBT agenda, allowed it to achieve the status of being "respectably queer" (Philipps 2014: 51). However, the expanding number of participants from over 4,000 in 2009 to 10,000 in 2011 (Philipps 2014: 51) and 20,000 in 2019 (https://pinkdot.sg) reveals that activists have succeeded in these trying circumstances to launch an "invented tradition" of an annual festival that calls attention to diversity. By 2016, the number of attendees grew to the tens of thousands (Yulius et al. 2018: 190).

Sex outside heterosexual marriage is illegal in Malaysia. Women's groups in Malaysia have respected the taboo on sexuality and have "shied away from such issues" (Ng et al. 2006: 131). Hence, the LGBT movement there is still very young, appearing only when it becomes socially acceptable to discuss sexual issues in the public sphere. Seksualiti Merdeka (Sexuality Independence), a loose non-institutionalized collection of individuals founded in 2008, has begun an annual sexuality rights festival using art exhibits, installations and performances to give audiences "a sense of belonging and community" (Lee 2012: 176). In 2010 it boasted an audience of 1,000 people over the three nights of the festival (Lee 2012: 176).

Unlike the Pink Dot festival, which continues to be celebrated at the time of writing, Seksualiti Merdeka (Malaysia's most well-known LGBT event; Ng 2018: 1100) has been banned since 2011, when a YouTube video appeared with a gay Muslim Malay man hoping Malaysians would one day be able to say "Saya gay, saya okay" ("I'm gay, I'm okay"). The video created a furore, with some religious authorities of Malaysia suggesting that the man should be arrested because his statement amounted to a "confession" of illegal sexual activity (Lee 2012: 179). The most prominent Malaysian LGBT advocacy organization, the Pink Triangle Foundation (PTF), provides telephone counseling on HIV/AIDS and sexuality and was registered as a foundation in 2000. PTF has initiated projects beyond the HIV/AIDS portfolio, attempting to organize national and regional networks of men who have sex with men (MSM) and transgender people to improve not just health but also sexual rights. However, once PTF attempted to expand its domain it received pressure from the Malaysian government to remain focused on its public health agenda (Ng 2018). Hence, these examples show that art festivals are acceptable only if they avoid mentioning the topic of sexuality/ies, and as long as no overt LGBT agenda is put forward. Given these limited parameters, activists have only been able to create some visibility but have not yet been allowed to tell their stories. Despite these challenges, the expanding number of participants in these events means that they have found audiences, and it is possible to build followers.

In contrast to Singapore and Malaysia, in the Philippines LGBT activists have succeeded in launching the first LGBT political party (and at the time of writing the only existing LGBT political party in the world) (Coloma 2013: 483). Since 1995 the Philippines has had a party-list system of elections which allows small political parties to represent the marginalized sectors, constituting 20 percent of the total number of the House of Representatives. In 2003, Ladlad (the word comes from Tagalog *magladlad*, which translates loosely as "to unfurl the cap used to cover one's body like a shield," but it also means "to come out of the closet") (Coloma 2013: 283–4) was founded as the "first national political party in the Philippines that focuses on the lesbian, gay, bisexual and transgender cause," hoping "to create a society that is gender-sensitive and free from all forms of sexual discrimination" (Coloma 2013: 490). It put forth candidates for the 2010 and 2013 elections but failed to get the necessary percentage of the votes to claim a seat in congress. However, it can boast the support of 114,120 people, or 0.39 percent of the party-list votes cast nationally. The party's election campaign and its outreach program resulted in the organization of regional chapters all over the country with the candidates visiting schools, town halls, wet markets, Miss Gay beauty pageants and so on, enabling the party to claim a visible space to educate the public about intolerance and discrimination against LGBT persons, and challenging the view that Filipinos are tolerant about sexual diversity (Coloma 2013).

Lambda Indonesia (LI), founded in 1982, is the first gay organization in Indonesia (Wijaya 2020: 39). It aimed to work towards disseminating the view that homosexuality was normal and something natural and to present more affirming views of homosexuality to help gay men "shed feelings of shame, fear and guilt" (Wijaya 2020: 40, 56). Even though LI disbanded in 1986, gay activists in the late 1980s and 1990s became involved in campaigning for issues such as HIV/AIDS and public health with the use of foreign funding (Wijaya 2020: 70). GAYa NUSANTARA was formed a year later and to this day advocates for the social acceptance of homosexuality and the empowerment of men with same-sex desires (Wijaya 2020: 71). Several lesbian activist organizations were set up between 2004 and 2006 focusing on the human rights of lesbian persons. Some of these include the Women's Rainbow Institute (Institut Pelangi Perempuan, IPP) and Pontianak's Tomboy Association (Persatuan Tomboy Pontianak, Pertopan). After 2005, lesbian activists formed LBT-INA, an umbrella organization for all organizations entitled LBT women, Lesbian and Bisexual, and Transgender Indonesia (LBT-INA). Arus Pelangi was founded to advocate for the rights of LGBT Indonesians through campaigns, policy advocacy and public education (Wijaya 2020: 132). All these activist organizations have pushed for greater awareness of sexual rights, and demanded that the state redress "queer injuries" or cases of discrimination and violence that LGBT persons have endured (Wijaya 2020: 133–36).

For Myanmar, the LGBT national organization VIVID was founded outside the country in Chiang Mai, Thailand in 2007. The activists returned to Yangon, Myanmar in 2013 to help other queer Burmese to shift "their understanding of queer suffering – that it should not be accepted or justified based on karma, but should be regarded as human rights violations for which somebody or something else is to blame – and by encouraging them to take up responsibility to the self and to queer Burmese collectively to fight for the remedy, human rights" (Chua 2018: 9). In the 2015 elections, the LGBT movement was able to expand to twenty grassroots locations around the country (Chua 2018: 3–4).

Have there been victories in the arena of legal change and the passage of anti-discrimination laws regarding sexual diversity? In Thailand, the NGO Anjaree succeeded in convincing the Thai Ministry of Health to remove homosexuality from its list of mental illnesses in 2002 (Sinnott 2011: 218). In July 2020, the Thai Cabinet approved a draft civil partnership bill together with a law that if passed would amend the Thai Civil Code and allow same-sex civil partnership (Muntarbhorn 2020). In Cambodia, LGBT persons were given recognition for the first time in the 2014 MoWA Cambodia Gender Assessment, and the National Action Plan to Prevent Violence Against Women does include violence against LGBT persons (Hoefinger et al. 2016: 323). In 2012, gay activist Déde Oetomo and prominent *waria* Mami Yuli ran for the commissioner post in the National Commission on Human Rights. Although neither succeeded in acquiring the position, Oetomo's comment that "I have *approached the state* as an openly gay man. Now, other LGBTI persons should make use of this opportunity and expand it" is clear evidence that activists have begun the process of "queering the idea of citizenship" and thus "demonstrating that LGBT people are legitimate citizens of Indonesia" (Wijaya 2020: 138–39).

Sayoni, a group focusing on advocacy for lesbians in Singapore, has been able to submit a report to the Commission on the Elimination of Discrimination Against Women (CEDAW) documenting the state policies that discriminate against sexual minorities in Singapore. CEDAW is one of the two international human rights conventions that the Singaporean government has ratified. The very fact that CEDAW's gender experts were in talks with the Singaporean government has been interpreted by Sayoni as an important victory for activists and as a first step in a public, international recognition of their concerns (Tang 2017: 114–15).

An anti-discrimination bill to protect the rights of LGBT persons has been filed in the Philippine 15th and 16th Congress, which "impose fines in cases of discrimination against LGBT people, including the disclosure of sexual orientation as a necessary criterion for the hiring, promotion, or dismissal of workers, refusal of admission to or expulsion from educational institutions on the basis of one's sexual orientation and gender identity, and denying access to LGBT people to health and other public facilities" (Das and Sharma 2016: 2). One must bear in mind that the LGBT movements in Southeast Asia are relatively young and that they face enormous challenges. The campaigns that they have launched to make citizens aware of LGBT issues using art, performance, workshops and social-cultural events have so far been successful in making their struggles visible as the first steps in gaining acceptance and public support.

5.6 Imagining Alternative Constructions of Gender and Sexuality: The Migration Context

The agency that Southeast Asians, particularly women, have to resist the heterosexual marriage imperative is severely limited by the way societies and states police sexualities, and the way religious authorities generate "moral panics" about attempts to alter the status quo. These conditions make it difficult for many Southeast Asians to think outside the box when it comes to gender and sexuality or to imagine a world that is more tolerant of gender diversity, let alone to radically reject hegemonic ideals. However, in an increasingly globalized world where Southeast Asians have become one of the most mobile people, migrating for work, for marriage or for the family, moving to new contexts provides many Southeast Asians with the opportunity (at least in these new spaces as "outsiders") to resist and reject conventional ideals on gender and sexuality and to fashion alternative models.

The moral surveillance of state and society fades when Southeast Asians migrate, most especially if they move to Western or Westernized countries. Free from the prying eyes of the village and the community, and free from restrictions generated by state laws (against homosexuality, for example), migrants feel that they can reinvent themselves. The Philippines is one of the largest labor-sending countries in the world, with 10 million people, or 10 percent of the population, working overseas. The feminization of Filipino migration since the 1970s and 1980s has meant that there are now both single and married Filipino women who have become breadwinners, and trail-blazers, extending the meaning of working outside the home to its most extreme parameters because they live in a different country from their families. The most radical way these women transgress gender ideals is by having sexual affairs or indulging in adultery while overseas. In their published memoirs, and using pseudonyms, Filipina domestic workers in Singapore openly admit to having had boyfriends (and sexual relationships) with Chinese, Bangladeshi, Sri Lankan, Indian and American men (Banados 2011). Most of these boyfriends are married men (Banados 2011). Since neither partner is single and divorce is illegal in the Philippines, the result is that they form short-term relationships, including one-day stands (rather than one-night stands, since workers only get one day off per week and the day off does not include the evening).

These women break several social taboos. First of all, women's open discussions about sexual matters (albeit using pseudonyms) is considered shocking in the Philippines. Second, the disclosure that women have several lovers reveals that they are behaving more like the masculine ideal rather than the feminine one. The title of one of these migrant stories – "A Childless 'Single Wife' Overseas" – means that they have even invented a new category to describe themselves – the single wife – and to explain their romantic lifestyles (Banados 2011: 58). Third, while men's infidelity is tolerated in Filipino society, women's adultery is not. The married woman with a lover is extremely rare in official representations of women. Thus, Filipina overseas workers' stories debunk the myth of the chaste wife. Finally, women know that their liaisons are not going to lead to forming new families. They are prohibited from accessing absolute divorce and cannot form new families with their new partners. The stories of these women migrants, who openly discuss their relationships with many men, constitute transgressive celebrations of female sexuality that break the link between women's sexual relations or emotional attachments and the ideal of creating a family (Roces 2021).

The topic of migration and lesbianism is still an under-researched topic in Filipino gender and migration studies although a handful of scholars have written about lesbianism among domestic workers in Hong Kong (Constable 2000: 221–47; Sim 2010: 37–50; Constable 2018). In a television news program, one Filipina estimates that a quarter of domestic workers in Hong Kong are lesbians (Constable 2000: 338). In the memoirs of Filipino women migrants, one claims she is not a lesbian although she has a female partner, while another does not consider sex with a woman a sign of unfaithfulness (underscoring traditional hegemonic beliefs that sex is imagined only heterosexually) (Banados 2011: 64–68). Yet, all the migrant women who reject the ideals of the chaste wife are effectively pioneers in dismantling traditional constructions of the feminine. By having sexual liaisons, heterosexual or not, and especially because these relationships are not imagined to be permanent, these married women are proclaiming that women have the right to sexual desire, and they are rejecting the Catholic Church's teachings that sex is confined to the marriage bed (Roces 2021).

In a pioneering major study of Filipino gay men in the diaspora, Martin Manalansan IV analyzes the way these "global divas" "find themselves in a liminal position in relation to mainstream white gay identity" (Manalansan IV 2006: 185). Nevertheless, these gay men fashion a space for themselves through linguistic markers such as *swardspeak* (their own language), and reclaim their Filipino *bakla* identity. To quote one of Manalansan's informants: "I used to think that I came to America to be gay, but then I realized I came to

America to be a real *bakla*" (Manalansan IV 2006: 97). According to Bobby Benedicto, *swardspeak* became a dying language in Manila and was considered unfashionable by the mid-2000s (Benedicto 2014: 78). When Filipino gay men in New York speak it, *swardspeak* reinforces the distinctiveness of these diasporic Filipinos from their counterparts in the homeland. Despite the challenges they face in a predominantly white society, Filipino gay men in New York acknowledge the fact that their very distance from Filipino society and their own families gives them the chance to become "global divas" (Manalansan IV 2006).

These migrant case studies illustrate that it is the escape from the surveillance of the state and the kinship group that enables Southeast Asians to challenge established cultural norms, giving them the space to imagine alternative constructions of sexuality. These can be incredibly radical, such as the new category of "the single wife," and liberating, such as for gay men in New York.

6 Power and Politics

6.1 Introduction

Women politicians are still a small minority all over Southeast Asia. The spectrum ranges from Myanmar, which is placed at the bottom of the gender equality index in Asia with less than 10 percent of parliamentary seats being held by women (Kyi 2018: 382), to the Philippines, where the figure is 30 percent. Does this mean that Southeast Asian politics is completely dominated by men and that women have been deprived of political power? This section analyzes the way political power is gendered in Southeast Asia, proposing that men's and women's roles in the kinship group define the rules for the gendering of politics. Furthermore, I suggest, the culture of kinship politics (defined here as utilizing political power for the benefit of the kinship alliance group) largely shapes the gendering of power. Southeast Asian concepts of power that see power held by the kinship alliance group and not just the person in office allow women the opportunity to exercise informal power behind the scenes, with access to power coming from their ties with men as wives, sisters, daughters and mothers of politicians. Ideal men are the patrons, the big men responsible for providing material wealth to the kinship group, while ideal women are supportive members of the group who work to promote their male candidate and are then rewarded with the "privilege" of exercising influence if he wins. In time, some of these women whose introduction to politics is typically campaigning for and supporting their male relatives may be able to transition to becoming politicians themselves. As long as women are the support system in kinship politics, the proverbial go-between, they will be relegated to exercising unofficial power rather than holding official power (Roces 1998: esp. ch. 2).

Through the years, Southeast Asia has boasted a number of high-profile women politicians holding the office of president or prime minister, so much so that the *Far Eastern Economic Review*, summarizing the usual way these women became politicians, joked that: "The avenues to political success are to choose one's father carefully, or a husband likely to be assassinated" (Ching 1993: 28). The humorous quip also captures the Southeast Asian view that women are imagined to be alter-egos of men. Indonesia's first female president Megawati Sukarnoputri is the daughter of former president Sukarno; President Gloria Macapagal of the Philippines is the daughter of former president Diosdado Macapagal; Prime Minister Yingluck Shinawatra is the sister of Thailand's former prime minister Thaksin Shinawatra; Myanmar's Aung San Suu Kyi is the daughter of nationalist leader Aung San; Corazon Aquino, the first female president of the Philippines, is the wife of assassinated opposition leader Benigno Aquino Jr.; Wan Azizah Wan Ismail, the first female deputy prime minister of Malaysia, is the wife of opposition figure and former deputy prime minister Anwar Ibrahim.

Wan Azizah's political story is illustrative of the wider trend. When her husband had a falling out with President Mahathir she declared publicly that she would take over the reform movement he led if he was ever arrested (Derichs 2013: 292). After his arrest, she formed the Parti Keadilan Nasional and won the constituency previously held by her husband in Penang State (Derichs 2013: 293–99). When Anwar Ibrahim was released from prison in 2004, he again became the de facto leader of the party. In her campaign for the 2008 election, Wan Azizah "publicly announced that she was going to stand as a proxy for Anwar" (Derichs 2013: 300). Wan Azizah Wan Ismail's role as "proxy" or "mouthpiece" of Anwar, who had "remote control" over his wife, is probably the most obvious example of the way women are viewed in politics – as alter-egos of men rather than as holding separate and unique identities themselves (Derichs 2013: 300, 309). Wives and female kin are therefore so closely identified with the candidate that as alter-egos they are seen to be their logical successors in political office. Women themselves are aware of this and are not ashamed to exploit this connection in their own bids for political power. In her early speeches, Aung San Suu Kyi, for example, periodically referred to herself as her father's daughter (Kyi 1995: 199; Harriden 2012: 209).

Using a case study of the Philippines with some examples from other parts of the region, this section demonstrates the way this gendering of politics plays out in practice. The division of gender roles where men are assigned the role of leaders of the kinship alliance group and women as supporters reinforces traditional androcentric constructions of women. The last part of the section summarizes the achievements of women's movements in helping pave the way for more women to play a role in formal politics and points out the challenges faced by those who advocate greater gender equality in politics.

6.2 Men in Office, Women behind the Scenes

In the Philippines, when a male candidate runs for office, he is expected to concentrate on delivering speeches and networking with local leaders and other male political leaders. On the other hand, his wife and female kin are responsible for organizing the supporters. They form women's support groups (e.g., Imelda Marcos had the Blue Ladies, composed of elite women from prominent families, to back her husband's first attempt at the presidency in 1965), are in charge of fundraising and are heavily involved in entertaining crowds at campaign rallies, an essential ingredient at elections. They look after the food preparation for political meetings and handle the door-to-door campaign (Roces 1998: 29–35). Once elected, the male politician is expected to act as patron in his bailiwick and concentrate on legislative duties. His wife and female kin are supposed to perform civic work and lead charitable organizations. For example, the wives of congressmen have been galvanized under the Congressional Spouses Foundation Inc. (CSFI) and the senators' wives are automatically members of the "Senate Ladies." Since 1986, both these organizations have been expected to run their own civic projects and charitable work. When the reverse is the case – that is, the woman is the politician and the man is the spouse – the male spouse usually sends a female such as a sister or daughter to represent him, revealing that these support groups are imagined to be gendered female. There are parallels of this Philippine example in other Southeast Asian contexts. In Myanmar, wives of government officials distributed medicine to poor mothers (Harriden 2012: 148) in the 1950s. During the Suharto era in Indonesia, it was compulsory for wives of civil servants to be members of the Dharma Wanita, an association established precisely to control the activities of these women, who were expected to support their husbands (Suryakusuma 1996: 92–119). Women's positions in the hierarchy of the organization paralleled their husband's position in the civil bureaucracy, that is, the wives of governors, district heads and subdistrict heads chaired the Dharma Wanita at those levels (Suryakusuma 1996: 99).

Wives and female kin are also expected to feed the constituents when they visit their husbands in their homes, since the custom is that people who seek help from their political representatives will visit them personally in their home. If a wife is not interested in fulfilling these roles or if the politician is not married, usually the mother, daughter or sister of the politician steps in. For example, in her younger years, Corazon Aquino preferred to concentrate on her role as housewife and mother and so it was her mother-in-law Doña Aurora Aquino who stepped into the active role of support system for her son, Senator Benigno Aquino Jr. Since Congressman Gerardo Roxas Jr., "Dinggoy," was a bachelor in 1987, it was his mother Judy Araneta Roxas (who had extensive experience as a senator's wife to Gerardo Roxas) who was the driving force behind the projects run by the Gerry Roxas Foundation – a formidable institution whose activities included scholarship grants, a Hublag Capiznon Money shop that gave liberalized credit to vendors, farmers, women, fisher folk, urban poor, cooperatives and community-based organizations, a microlending project and even Capiz Women Inc., which addressed women's issues and had 3,800 members in 1995 (Roccs 1998: 60–61). Yet despite, all these activities, the golden rule for these women is not to claim credit for any of their work behind the scenes. Mrs. Roxas was self-effacing, claiming that her sons (when Dinggoy died, his brother Mar, then also a bachelor, succeeded him as congressman and later senator) won their positions through their own merits: "I'm just extra there" (Roxas 1995, interview with author). In a newspaper interview, she stressed: "I have nothing to do with the political work in Capiz. I draw a line separating the foundation from politics" (Roces 1998: 60–61). In the 1990s she would go to Capiz (in the central Philippines, the Roxas family bailiwick) every weekend, attending to the civic work of the foundation. Although she remains the person most responsible for building and maintaining the congressional career of her sons, she assumes the traditional pose – that she is not really very important and that she dwells only in the background, the acceptable space where women may exercise power (Roces 1998: 61).

The power behind the scenes that women can access, however, is very real power. The best example of its enormous potential is found in the career of former first lady Imelda Romualdez Marcos, who succeeded in pushing this power to its limits and then later on claimed political office herself. Mrs. Marcos was of course first lady during a dictatorship (1972–86); the fact that the regime suppressed political opposition gave her more room and scope to exercise power unchallenged by critics. Nevertheless, she took the role of first lady as civic worker and patron of the arts and culture to unparalleled heights. She launched a nationwide beautification campaign, built a village of youth for orphans with money she solicited from wealthy families, raised money for several hospitals, built the Cultural Centre, the Maligayang Pasko Parks and the Nayong Pilipino (a tourist village showing miniature replicas of the country's tourist spots as well as presenting Philippine traditional arts and crafts) and she enlarged the Christmas gift-giving drives, to name a few of her projects before martial law was declared in 1972. During the subsequent years of the dictatorship she launched construction projects of voluminous proportion, including the building of the longest bridge in the Philippines in 1974, the San Juanico Bridge, which linked the two relatively undeveloped islands of Leyte and Samar. She built the Folk Arts Theatre, several tourist hotels, the Manila Film Center, the Coconut Palace (originally for the pope's intended visit), the Palace in the Sky in Tagaytay and hospitals such as the Philippine Heart Center, the Lung Center, the Kidney Center and the Lungsod ng Kabataan, or Children's City (Roces 1998: 45–46). She organized the Nutrition Center of the Philippines and developed the Research Institute for Tropical Medicine (RITM) in Alabang Muntinlupa (Manapat 1991: 278). Invading the field of education, she built and inaugurated her very own University of Life (Roces 1998: 46). The fact that the Philippines during the martial law period (1972–86) is described by journalist Primitivo Mijares as the "conjugal dictatorship of Ferdinand and Imelda Marcos" (Mijares 1976) underscores the co-equal status and power of the president and the first lady.

The danger, of course, is that from the Western perspective such power is illegitimate and undemocratic. Most Filipinos, too, were critical of Mrs. Marcos' unprecedented exercise of power behind the scenes. In 1993, a major scandal forced the informal power exercised by women close to the president into the open, when a two-part newspaper article series run by the Centre for Investigative Journalism asserted that Mrs. Rosemarie Arenas, alleged former mistress of then President Fidel Ramos, was using her past relationship with the president to exercise influence in government. This included accusations that she used her close connection to the presidency to boost certain businesses, influence government appointments, facilitate shipments with the Bureau of Customs, acquire duty-free concessions for friends and host a Wednesday Club gathering at her home with officials close to the president to plot political strategies (Danguilan-Vitug and Gloria 1993: 1, 12–13). The series argued that Arenas' power was "both real and perceived" and her defence that she was merely "helping" and not "meddling" simply affirmed that she did interfere in political matters (Danguilan-Vitug and Gloria 1993: 1, 12–13; Gloria and Danguilan-Vitug 1993: 1 and 10).

This case study of the Philippines has parallels in other Southeast Asian countries. In Cambodia, "a woman's authority is determined by her kin relationships with male power figures" and "wives of male leaders are viewed as especially powerful and they are expected to act in the interests of the family clan" (Frieson 2001: 3). These women who have ruled "in the shadows" (Frieson 2001) include Lon Nol's first wife, Princess Monique (King Sihanouk's wife) and Khieum Ponnary (Pol Pot's first wife), who are all alleged to have influenced from behind the scenes (Frieson 2001: 3). In early postcolonial Burma, wives of Anti-Fascist People's Freedom League (AFPFL; the main political alliance in Burma from 1945 to 1958) leaders exercised political influence "both through and over their husbands" (Harriden 2012: 156). Even in the later period of military rule in Burma (from 1962 onwards), women with close ties to the Burmese military are believed to have exercised enormous influence in the political and economic sphere (Harriden 2012: 42, 191; Williams 2001: 186–87). General Ne Win's daughter Sandar Win has wielded enormous wealth and political power. The source of her influence has been her unique position as the link between lower military officers, the BSPP parliament and her father. A physician by training, she is the only woman to hold a senior position in the army, as a major in the medical corps due to her qualification as a physician (Harriden 2012: 191). Mrs. Suharto of Indonesia had enormous influence on "the fate of high-ranking government officials who [. . .] committed 'sexual transgressions' such as divorce or polygamy, though these are legal acts" (Suryakusuma 1996: 104). In Indonesia during the New Order the women who held appointed seats in parliament were often spouses or relatives of powerful men (Robinson 2018: 312).

Exercising power behind the scenes through links with male politicians is one clear pathway for a woman to make a career in politics (Roces 1998; Choi 2019). Most Burmese women who have been elected to parliament or have been active in insurgent movements have been wives or relatives of male leaders (Harriden 2012). Historian Trude Jacobsen argues that women without connections with male politicians are unlikely to enter the Cambodian political sphere (Jacobsen 2008: 260). She cites the following prominent examples: (1) Princess Vacheahra (half-sister to King Sihanouk), a member of parliament for Siem Reap in 1998 and Phnom Penh in 2003 (Jacobsen 2008: 260); (2) Princess Sisowath Santa (granddaughter of King Norodom), elected to the National Assembly in 1998 and 2004; (3) Princess Norodom Rattanadevi, a member of parliament for Kratie; and (4) Tiuolong Saumura, wife of Sam Rainsy (the son of Sam Sary, former deputy prime minister and minister of finance), elected twice as a member of parliament for Phnom Penh (Jacobsen 2008: 260–61). Yingluck Shinawatra also became Thai prime minister through her connections with her brother, former Thai prime minister Thaksin Shinawatra (Bjarnegård 2013: 92).

The results of the 2019 elections in Indonesia reveal that almost half (44 percent) of female candidates elected to Indonesia's national parliament were members of political dynasties – meaning to say that the women had family connections as wives, daughters or sisters of political officeholders or party leaders (Wardani and Subekti 2021). The case study of West Sumatra in that same election round provides some explanation for this clear gender divide. Since Indonesia's 2003 Election Law introduced a 30-percent quota of women candidates, political parties approached the wives of politicians in West Sumatra to persuade them to run for election and therefore take advantage of their husbands' networks and political influence (Kabullah and Fajri 2021). Thus, while it may appear on paper that there is much to rejoice in the rise in the quantity of women elected to political office in Indonesia, the method through which they gained this power "further emphasises how party elites, at least, saw these women as accessories of their husbands" (Kabullah and Fajri 2021).

In democratic regimes, term limits for officeholders are likely to increase the number of women in politics. If a male politician is restricted to only two or three consecutive terms in office, then to prolong the hold of the kinship alliance group on office his wife will be pressured to run for office and take his place after his term is up. The members of the Lady Mayors' Association in the Philippines even refer to themselves as "breakers," a term that connotes their roles as proxies running for office simply to "break" the term of office of their husbands or male kin (Tapales 2002: 54). Once the intermission or "break" is over, their husbands will once again run for office.

The most interesting example so far that demonstrates the resiliency of this women's pathway to political power is the example of Geraldine Roman, who in 2016 became the first transgender woman elected to the Philippine House of Representatives. Roman's success is not connected to the LGBT activist movement as she did not run in the party list of Ladlad. She is actually one of the female "breakers" discussed above since she succeeded her mother, who exhausted her term limit, and her late father, who had previously held the congressional seat for the first district of Bataan, a city 120 kilometers from Manila. Roman does not call attention to her (trans)gender identity and did not promote LGBT issues as her main concern during her election campaign. Since she had sex reassignment surgery in the 1990s and is married to a man, is Catholic and is supported by her family, she is "deemed a 'real' woman" (Coloma forthcoming). This case demonstrates that transgender women have been able to access political power if, like other women, they access power through kinship ties with male politicians and continue the family "dynasty."

Elin Bjarnegård introduces the concept of homosocial capital to explain why it is more difficult for women to enter formal politics in Thailand (Bjarnegård 2013). Homosocial capital is formed through informal networking and women are disadvantaged because this essential networking takes place in arenas where women are excluded, such as karaoke bars, massage parlors and so on – places where it is acceptable for men to meet but which are not women-friendly spaces (Bjarnegård 2013: 92–94). While these are popular business leisure pursuits men indulge in, women have to be "very careful with drinking, gambling, and having affairs, for instance [. . .] since women will be immediately discredited if they do any of this. Women are watched much more carefully and always have to behave nicely" (Bjarnegård 2013: 165). As one of Bjarnegård's informants put it: "How do you do it if they do not drink cognac and play golf?" (Bjarnegård 2013: 169). If a female candidate dares to participate in these male spaces, she risks gossip about possible inappropriate romantic liaisons with the men she is socializing with, possibly tarnishing her reputation as a "chaste" woman and damaging her chances of getting elected.

But there is more than one pathway to women's political advancement in Southeast Asia. Nankyung Choi identifies three: an elite pathway, which refers to women's links with elite male politicians described above; a grassroots pathway, in which women build a track record as communal leaders, mediators of public services or village heads; and a "middle pathway," which refers to "the pursuit of politics as a vocation through entrepreneurial experimentation with a diversity of strategies for acquiring and maintaining political power" (Choi 2019: 242). Thus, clearly access to kinship politics is not the only pathway by which women can enter politics, although it is still the dominant one.

A sterling example of the "grassroots pathway" is the number of women leaders of NGOs and prominent women's organizations who have made it to political office. The feminist organization GABRIELA runs its own women's party in the Philippines (GABRIELA Women's Party) through which it is possible for candidates to compete in party lists. Since 2004, four GABRIELA candidates, all of whom have had a track record with leadership roles within that organization prior to entering formal politics, have become congresswomen (Liza Maza, Luzviminda Ilagan, Emerenciana de Jesus and Arelene Brosas). When I interviewed Emerenciana (Emmi) de Jesus in 2003, she was deputy director of GABRIELA (de Jesus 2003, interview with author). By 2010, she had succeeded in winning a congressional seat representing the GABRIELA women's party list.

The middle pathway may incorporate professionals like Supreme Court Justice Cecilia Muñoz Palma, who metamorphosed into a parliamentarian (with the Batasan Pambasa) as an opposition candidate against the Marcos-controlled Congress in 1984 (Roces 1998: 143). This middle pathway can also include celebrities, movie stars, television journalists and presenters who have been able to translate their popularity to electoral votes. Before entering politics, Senators Loren Legarda, Risa Hontiveros-Baraquiel and Nikki Coseteng had careers as television presenters (Roces 2012: 158). Their reputation as feminist journalists and the fact that they were practically household names as television stars gave them the exposure needed to get votes and they were elected without needing to have ties with male politicians.

Once entering politics, women still face the challenge of "navigating a man's world," to quote the subtitle of a recent book on women and politics in Southeast Asia (Devasahayam 2019). In Singapore, women parliamentarians have to juggle the triple burden of professional career, politics and family responsibilities and therefore do not take the plunge unless they have discussed it with their families (Devasahayam 2019: 17–39). Female legislators also have to resort to using gendered practices such as appealing to male gallantry and using female charm such as *cariño* or *lambing* (both Tagalog terms referring to mannerisms of endearment) to garner support from male colleagues when they propose legislation. This is a counterpoint to male politicians' gendered networking techniques such as drinking alcohol (not usually practiced by Southeast Asian women) and playing golf together (Roces 1998: 104; Bjarnegärd 2013). In a context where female politicians are a minority and need the backing of colleagues to pass legislation, they also have to tread carefully so as not to upstage their male counterparts or damage their male self-esteem (*amor propio*) (Roces 1998: 105).

6.3 Activism and Gender Advocacy in the Realm of Politics

What have feminist activists achieved in the realm of politics? What have they done to alter laws to enable more women to enter formal politics and/or improve the situation of women? Have they tried to change men and women's roles in the kinship group or Southeast Asian concepts of power? This section will assess the track record in these projects.

One of the main issues that feminist activists hope to lobby for is to increase the number of women politicians so that they no longer are the minority. In Indonesia this has succeeded somewhat with the passage in 2004 of an electoral quota of 30 percent for women legislators, including a "zipper" system requiring at least one woman to be placed within the top three of the lists of political parties (Satriyo 2010: 243; Robinson 2014: 52). However, local women politicians in Indonesia do not necessarily have a program for women's issues (Dewi 2015). Clearly, activists also need to work on getting politicians elected who are gender-sensitive, rather than simply gaining more female numbers in parliament. Across the region, some have already started to address this need. In Cambodia, prior to the 2003 elections, two NGOs, Women in Prosperity and the Women's Association for Peace and Development, were founded precisely to encourage women to stand for election and to give them the required education and training necessary to launch these new careers (Jacobsen 2010: 217). In Indonesia, in 2012, the Ministry of Women's Empowerment and Child Protection together with the United Nations Development Program (UNDP) established Strengthening Women's Participation and Representation in Governance in Indonesia (SWARGA) to increase women's participation in parliament in the 2014 elections, as well as "to strengthen the capacity of women parliamentarians" (Hilman 2017: 44). SWARGA ran training programs for candidates and MPs and funded activities to bolster the Women's Parliamentary Caucus (Kaukus Perempuan Parlemen, KPP), and even crated a national Women's Parliamentary Network to support women MPs (Hilman 2017: 45). The challenge, of course, is that even though programs coordinated by the Indonesian government and international donors succeed in increasing the pool of qualified (and even gender-sensitive) female candidates, the biggest hurdle is to convince political parties to recruit these women. Ben Hilman's study reveals that political parties are more interested in women with money than women with talent and prefer to choose female candidates who are wives of established politicians (Hilman 2017: 45–46).

Another glaring issue in politics is that there is as yet no women's vote (women do not vote for a woman politician just because she is a woman) (Roces 2012; Satriyo 2010: 261). Perhaps it might be a good idea for feminists to build one. After all, one can argue that the women's organizations in the Philippines have already been successful in building a mass following. It is difficult to measure the composition of the Filipino women's movements in quantitative terms because membership fluctuates over the years and there is also the question of whether or not we should include in the tally the audiences of feminist television and radio shows, or theatre, performance events, rallies and demonstrations. GABRIELA, for example, could boast a membership of 50,000 in 2006 (Roces 2012). In Indonesia, the leftist women's organization GERWANI had acquired a huge mass following (from 100,000 in 1957 to 1.5 million in 1963) prior to 1965 (Blackburn 2004: 178) but was completely decimated after the 1965–66 massacre of communists in the aftermath of the coup d'état that brought Suharto to power. Indonesia's feminist movement has not been able rebuild such membership numbers; however, the rise of Islamic feminism, which blossomed in the 1990s, has been able to give Indonesian feminism one kind of mass-based women's organization and that is the Islamic one (Blackburn 2010: 28–29).

It is possible for feminists to utilize the membership of their organizations in the project of fashioning a woman's vote. This mass following, however, still needs to be built in countries such as Singapore, Cambodia and Malaysia (Ng et al. 2006: 7, 61; Jacobsen 2010: 218; Lyons 2010). Singapore has been criticized for having only a one-organization women's movement with the acronym AWARE (Association for Women for Action and Research) (Lyons 2010: 84–87). But in 2009, when a group of Christian women attempted to seize the leadership of AWARE, the power struggle compelled both camps (dubbed the old guard and the new guard) to mobilize supporters and the membership soared from a waning 300 to a respectable 3,000 just before the extraordinary meeting organized to produce a no-confidence vote to depose the new guard (Chong 2011: 2). In the case of Malaysia, women's groups have been able to become more visible and have been more confident in engaging with the state (Ng et al. 2006: 70–71).

However, activists should be applauded for making enormous gains in raising awareness on taboo issues such as sexual rights and domestic violence, rape and incest. Removing the taboos and airing these issues in public has helped generate pro-women legislation. In Indonesia and the Philippines, activists have been able to outlaw domestic violence and include marital rape in the anti-rape laws (Robinson 2008: 181; Roces 2012). While the Domestic Violence Act of 1994 in Malaysia prohibits a man to beat his wife, it does not punish him for marital rape (Ng et al. 2006: 51–52). However, Ng et al. argue that the campaign against domestic violence united both Muslims and non-Muslims and succeeded in "stealing some thunder from the Syariah courts" since "the law transcended the jurisdiction of Syariah laws over Muslim family matters where domestic violence was concerned, something that was unprecedented in Malaysia" (Ng et al. 2006: 55). An Anti-Trafficking in Persons Law passed in the Philippines in 2003 absolves prostituted women of criminal acts and instead criminalizes the perpetrators (Roces 2012: 62–63). An anti-sexual harassment law was passed in the Philippines (Act 7877) in 1995.

The challenge for feminists today is to think about how to deal with the stigma and controversial aspects associated with the kinds of women who exercise unofficial power through their kinship ties to powerful men. Should activists also devote their energies into tapping the talents of these very capable wives and kin of male politicians and launch a strategy to imbue them with a feminist perspective? These women clearly exercise power behind the scenes, but generally have not been tapped into the women's movements.

Finally, activists also need to deconstruct the links between gender and the kinship alliance group. This is extremely challenging because this project involves critiquing Southeast Asian concepts of power. I am also ambivalent about this since these concepts of power allow women to exercise informal power and as long as women politicians are the minority, would it be wise to remove another avenue of influence from them, despite the stigma associated with kinship politics and women's role as support mechanism for the kinship group? Nonetheless, there is still a pressing need for an educational campaign that challenges the cultural requirement that women be attached to men in order to access political power.

7 Conclusion

To conclude this Element, I want to underscore how gender specialists working on Southeast Asia have challenged assumptions proposed by scholars working in gender studies in Western contexts. I end with suggestions for future research, and my assessment of what questions have yet to be posed or addressed by gender activists in the region. While these may look like separate projects, many gender scholars based in Southeast Asia are very much plugged into the activist movements there (Roces 2010; 2012). At the same time, activists in the region are connected to global movements that are influenced by gender theorizing in the global North while using their personal links (including funding sources) to lobby for gender rights in their countries.

So how have scholars working on Southeast Asia contributed to the field of gender studies? Responding to Maila Stivens' call to expand the conceptual domain of what we define as "politics," scholars have examined women's informal power behind the scenes as spouses and relatives of men in political and religious leadership spheres (Roces 1998; Smith and Woodward 2014; Frisk 2009; Harriden 2012; Kloos 2019). They have focused on how concepts of spiritual potency and power add a new dimension to understanding the fashioning of gender hierarchies.

Scholars have also modified Western-derived theoretical work on sexualities in adapting it to the Southeast Asian context. Michael Peletz introduces the concept of "gender pluralism" to describe the way multiple genders have traditionally been constructed in Southeast Asia in a manner distinct from Western constructs; he suggests that, over time and due to changing historical contexts including colonialism and modernity, societies have become less tolerant and less gender-pluralist (Peletz 2006). Scholars have shown that gender categories do not automatically translate across regions, illustrating, for example, that specifically Southeast Asian terms, like "dee" and "tom" in Thai and *tomboy*, hunter, *calalai* and *cewek* in Indonesia, are alternative conceptual categories that do not translate to the Western term of "lesbian" (Sinnott 2004; Blackwood 2010; Davies 2007).

Saskia Wieringa's (2015a) brilliant intervention is to suggest an alternative to queer theory by suggesting that it is heteronormativity – "a double-edged sword that not only marginalizes those who fall outside its norms but also patrols those within its constraints" (Wieringa et al. 2015: 27) – that explains why certain groups of people suffer terrible discrimination. The model of heteronormativity, passionate aesthetics and symbolic subversion that Wieringa proposes is very useful in explaining not just the marginalization of women who love women, but also the marginalization (described by them as being "reduced to mud") experienced by other categories of women who are not attached to men, such as divorced women, sex workers, widows and single women. Wieringa's model is particularly powerful because it does not separate women who love women from other women who suffer stigma simply because they are not attached to a heterosexual man. In her view, these marginalized actors use the methods of passionate aesthetics and symbolic subversion to challenge the "formidable symbolic power" of heteronormativity in the national arena of sexual politics (Wieringa et al. 2015: 31–35). These forms of resistance are symbolic, involving "secrecy, partial acceptance of the codes of normalcy, denial of personal needs, and the secret search for sexual pleasure" as well as "hard work, sacrifice and defiance" (Wieringa et al. 2015: 35). This interpretive model arising from Wieringa's empirical research in India and Indonesia is a prime example of the way the Southeast Asian context (and indeed the larger Asian context) can make important contributions to the field of gender and sexualities studies beyond the region.

While the number of publications on the theme of cultural constructions of gender in Southeast Asia continue to increase, revealing that the field is healthy and robust, there are still many under-researched areas. As I have noted, the biggest vacuum is men and masculinities. Scholars are also beginning to grapple with the way migration has altered gender constructs and more of this should be encouraged. Globalization in the form of migration is one important source of changes in gender ideals since when men and women move away from the prying eyes of the state, religious organizations and, most importantly, the kinship group, they can find the space and the opportunities to imagine alternatives. Finally, there is also a need for more gender studies research on East Timor, Laos and the many diverse ethnic minority groups in the region (such as the pioneering work of Resurrección (1999) and Mikkelsen (2018) on the Kalungaya and the Bugkalot of the Philippine Cordillera).

Turning to the state of gender advocacy, it is obvious that women's movements have been successful in launching major critiques of cultural constructions of women and advocating for change by using the language of human rights and tapping their transnational connections. However, there is much still to be done. In particular, women's movements and gender advocates in general have yet to seriously challenge cultural constructions of the masculine, and male heterosexuality. There is a need for more campaigns such as that launched by the Coalition Against Trafficking in Women-Asia Pacific (CATW-AP) in 2006 entitled "real men don't buy women," which was an attempt to curb prostitution by challenging men's perceived rights to visit prostitutes and have mistresses (Roces 2012: 61). Activists still need to launch campaigns to alter the association of virility and masculine ideals. So far, the fight for LGBT rights has been a battle for the inclusion of alternative sexualities, rather than a plea for the reform of hegemonic masculinities.

One of the cultural constructions of the feminine that activists have not yet been able to seriously contest is the ideal woman as beauty queen. It is necessary to dismantle the link between physical beauty and female virtue and morality because it motivates women to focus on their physical appearance as a priority rather than developing their leadership or intellectual talents.

While the project of altering constructions of gender is still a work in progress, activists have already began to propose alternative role models for women. These include women as interpreters of the Qur'an, women as leaders of organizations and women as workers, all important because they not only pronounce that women can now enter roles previously dominated by men, but also because they suggest that women are not limited to the traditional and entrenched ideal of the wife and mother. In the Philippine case, they have proposed the pre-Hispanic priestess (*babaylan*) who is a wise woman past menopause age as a role model for all Filipino women. This idea is radical since the woman as scholar/intellectual has never been in the purview of definitions of the feminine in contemporary Southeast Asia.

Finally, activists still need to grapple with the marriage imperative (Boellstorff 2005) or, to be more accurate, the heteronormative marriage imperative. The cultural view that adulthood is achieved only with heterosexual marriage marginalizes both men and women who feel pressured to marry simply to avoid family shame or to be socially accepted. Although same-sex marriage is being debated in some countries, even if it is passed it will still endorse the institution of marriage. There needs to be some cultural campaign that will underscore the view that marriage is not the only rite of passage to adulthood.

This Element has analyzed cultural constructions of gender in Southeast Asia through the themes of gender ideals, religion and sexualities. It has examined the way authoritarian states have been able to fashion the feminine and the masculine and the way power and politics is gendered. One clear pattern that emerges from the region is that cultural constructions of gender can be very resilient and constraining. But activists have been able to begin the process of initiating fundamental changes. The literature on Southeast Asia also provides us with enormous insights into how cultural constructions of gender change over time and how activists have provided pathways to human fulfillment.

References

Afrianty, Dina (2015). *Women and Sharia Law in Northern Indonesia: Local Women's NGOs and the Reform of Islamic Law in Aceh*. London: Routledge.

Aguilar, Mila (2006). Babaylan, Tumanda Ka Na. In Fe Mangahas and Jenny R. Llaguno (eds.), *Centennial Crossings: Readings on Babaylan Feminism in the Philippines*. Quezon City: C & E Publishing, pp. 173–74.

Andaya, Barbara (2018). Gender Legacies and Modern Transitions. In Robert W. Hefner (ed.), *Routledge Handbook of Contemporary Indonesia*. London: Routledge, pp. 31–42.

Andaya, Barbara (2008). *The Flaming Womb: Repositing Women in Early Modern Southeast Asia*. Honolulu: University of Hawaii Press.

Andaya, Barbara (ed.) (2001). *Other Pasts: Women, Gender and History in Early Modern Southeast Asia*. Honolulu: Center for Southeast Asian studies, University of Hawaii.

Andaya, Leonard Y. (2000). The Bissu: A Study of a Third Gender in Indonesia. In Barbara Andaya (ed.), *Other Pasts: Women, Gender and History in Early Modern Southeast Asia*. Honolulu: University of Hawaii Press, pp.27–46.

Atkinson, Jane Monnig (1990). How Gender Makes a Difference in Wana Society. In Jane Monnig Atkinson and Shelly Errington (eds.), *Power and Difference: Gender in Island Southeast Asia*. Stanford, CA: Stanford University Press, pp.59–93.

Atkinson, Jane Monnig and Errington, Shelly (eds.) (1990). *Power and Difference: Gender in Island Southeast Asia*. Stanford, CA: Stanford University Press.

Araneta, Gemma Cruz (2018). What It is Like. *The Philippine Star*. July 15. www.philstar.com/lifestyle/sunday-life/2018/07/15/1833492/what-it-like.

Arriola, Fe Capellan (1989). *Si Maria, Nena, Gabriela Atbp*. Manila: GABRIELA and Institute of Women's Studies.

Badran, Margot (2002). Islamic Feminism: What's in a Name? *Al-Ahram Weekly Online*, January 17–23, issue 569. www.feministezine.com/femin ist/international/Islamic-Feminism-01.html.

Baird, Marian, Ford, Michele and Hill, Elizabeth (2017). *Women, Work and Care in the Asia-Pacific*. London: Routledge.

Banados, Papias Generale (2011). *The Path to Remittance: Tales of Pains and Gains of Overseas Filipino Workers*. Singapore: Global Eye Media.

Basarudin, Azza (2016). *Humanizing the Sacred: Sisters in Islam and the Struggle for Gender Justice in Malaysia*. Seattle: University of Washington Press.

Benedicto, Bobby (2014). *Under Bright Lights: Gay Manila and the Global Scene*. Minneapolis: University of Minnesota Press.

Bennett, Linda Rae (2005). *Islam and Modernity: Single Women, Sexuality and Reproductive Health in Contemporary Indonesia*. London: Routledge.

Bennet, Linda Rae and Davies, Sharyn Graham (eds.) (2015). *Sex and Sexualities in Contemporary Indonesia: Sexual Politics, Health Diversity and Representations*. London: Routledge.

Bjarnegård, Elin (2013). *Gender, Informal Institutions and Political Recruitment: Explaining Male Dominance in Parliamentary Presentation*. Basingstoke: Palgrave Macmillan.

Blackburn, Susan (2010). Feminism and the Women's Movement in the World's Largest Islamic Nation. In Mina Roces and Louise Edwards (eds.), *Women's Movements in Asia: Feminisms and Transnational Activism*. London: Routledge, pp. 21–33.

Blackburn, Susan (2004). *Women and the State in Indonesia*. Cambridge: Cambridge University Press.

Blackwood, Evelyn (2010). *Falling into the Lesbi World: Desire and Difference in Indonesia*. Honolulu: University of Hawaii Press.

Blackwood, Evelyn (1999). Tombois in West Sumatra: Constructing Masculinity and Erotic Desire. In Evelyn Blackwood and Saskia E. Wieringa (eds.), *Female Desires: Same-Sex Relations and Transgender Practices Across Cultures*. New York: Columbia University Press, pp. 181–205.

Blackwood, Evelyn (2007). Transnational Sexualities in One Place: Indonesian Readings. In Saskia E. Wieringa, Evelyn Blackwood and Abha Bhaiya (eds.), *Women's Sexualities and Masculinities in a Globalizing Asia*. New York: Palgrave Macmillan, pp. 181–99.

Boellstorff, Tom (2005). *The Gay Archipelago: Sexuality and Nation in Indonesia*. Princeton, NJ: Princeton University Press.

Leong, Lawrence Wai-Teng (2012). Asian Sexuality or Singapore Exceptionalism? *Liverpool Law Review*, 33, 11–26.

Brenner, Suzanne (1998). *The Domestication of Desire: Women, Wealth and Modernity in Java*. Princeton, NJ: Princeton University Press.

Brenner, Suzanne (1995). Why Women Rule the Roost: Rethinking Javanese Ideologies of Gender and Self-Control. In Aihwa Ong and Michael G. Peletz (eds.), *Bewitching Women, Pious Men: Gender and Body Politics in Southeast Asia*. Berkeley: University of California Press, pp. 26–50.

Bricknell, Katherine (2011). "We Don't Forget the Old Rice Pot When We Get the New One": Discourses on Ideals and Practices of Women in Contemporary Cambodia. *Signs*, 36(2), 437–62.

Cepeda, Mara. (2016). Alvarez: OK to Show De Lima's Alleged Sex Tape in House Probe. *Rappler*. September 28. www.rappler.com/nation/alvarez-show-de-lima-sex-tape-house-probe. Accessed December 7, 2020.

Chan, Jasmine (2000). The Status of Women in a Patriarchal State: The Case of Singapore. In Louise Edwards and Mina Roces (eds.), *Women in Asia: Tradition, Modernity, and Globalisation*. Sydney: Allen & Unwin, pp. 39–58.

Ching, Frank (1993). Asia's Women Leaders Depend on Parents' or Husbands' Fame. *Far Eastern Economic Review*, August 19, p. 28.

Chiricosta, Alexandra (2010). Following the Trail of the Fairy-Bird: The Search for a Uniquely Vietnamese Women's Movement. Mina Roces and Louise Edwards (eds.), *Women's Movements in Asia: Feminisms and Transnational Activism*. London: Routledge, pp. 124–43.

Choi, Nankyung (2019). Women's Political Pathways in Southeast Asia. *International Feminist Journal of Politics*, (21)2, 224–48.

Chong, Terence (2011). *Introduction*. In Terence Chong (ed.), *The AWARE Saga: Civil Society and Public Morality in Singapore*. Singapore: NUS Press.

Chua, Lynette J. (2018). *The Politics of Love in Myanmar: LGBT Mobilization and Human Rights as a Way of Life*. Stanford, CA: Stanford University Press.

Clark, Marshall (2010). *Maskulinitas: Culture, Gender and Politics in Indonesia*. Caulfield, VA: Monash University Press.

Collantes, Christianne F. (2018). *Reproductive Dilemmas in Metro-Manila: Faith, Intimacies and Globalization*. Singapore: Palgrave Macmillan.

Coloma, Ronald Sintos (forthcoming). The Struggle Continues: On the Cruel Optimism of LGBT Organizing. In Martin F. Manalansan IV, Rolando B. Tolentino and Robert G. Diaz (eds.), *Beauty and Brutality: Manila and its Global Discontents*. Durham, NC: Duke University Press.

Coloma, Ronald Sintos (2013). Ladlad and Parrhesiastic Pedagogy: Unfurling LGBT Politics and Education in the Global South. *Curriculum Inquiry*, 43(4), 483–511.

Constable, Nicole (2018). Assemblages and Affect: Migrant Mothers and the Varieties of Absent Children. *Global Networks*, 18(1), 168–85.

Constable, Nicole (2000). Dolls, T-Birds, and Ideal Workers. In Kathleen M. Adams and Sarah Dickey (eds.), *Home and Hegemony: Domestic Service and Identity Politics in South and Southeast Asia*. Ann Arbor: University of Michigan Press, pp. 221–47.

Cook, Nerida (1998). "Dutiful Daughters", Estranged Sisters: Women in Thailand. In Krishna Sen and Maila Stivens (eds.), *Gender and Power in Affluent Asia*. London: Routledge, pp. 250–90.

Creak, Simon (2015). *Embodied Nation: Sport, Masculinity and the Making of Modern Laos*. Honolulu: University of Hawaii Press.

Creese, Helen (2004). *Women of the Kakawin World: Marriage and Sexuality in the Indic Courts of Java and Bali*. Armonk, NY: M.E. Sharpe.

Danguilan-Vitug, Marites and Gloria, Glenda (1993). Past Relationships Impinges on Present Affairs of State. *Philippine Daily Inquirer*, October 11, pp. 1, 12–13.

Das, Arpita and Alankaar Sharma (2016). LGBT Activism in Southeast Asia. In Nancy A. Naples (ed.), *The Wiley Blackwell Encyclopedia of Gender and Sexuality Studies*. Malden, MA: Wiley & Sons, pp. 1–5 (online).

Davies, Sharyn Graham (2018). Skins of Morality: Bio-borders, Ephemeral Citizenship and Policing Women in Indonesia. *Asian Studies Review*, 42(1), 69–88.

Davies, Sharyn Graham (2015). Surveiling Sexuality in Indonesia. In Linda Rae Bennett and Sharyn Graham Davies (eds.), *Sex and Sexualities in Contemporary Indonesia: Sexual Politics, Health, Diversity and Representation*. London: Routledge, pp. 29–50.

Davies, Sharyn Graham (2010). *Gender Diversity in Indonesia. Sexuality, Islam and Queer Selves*. London: Routledge.

Davies, Sharyn Graham (2007). *Challenging Gender Norms: Five Genders among the Bugis in Indonesia*. Belmont, CA: Thomson Wadsworth.

Davies, Sharyn Graham and Bennett, Linda Rae (2015). Introduction: Mapping Sex and Sexualities in Contemporary Indonesia. In Linda Rae Bennett and Sharyn Graham Davies (eds.), *Sex and Sexualities in Contemporary Indonesia: Sexual Politics, Health, Diversity and Representation*. London: Routledge, pp. 1–26.

Davies, Sharyn Graham and Savitri, Harsono (2015). The Pretty Imperative: Handcuffing Policewomen in Indonesia. *Intersections: Gender and Sexuality in Asia and the Pacific*, 37. http://intersections.anu.edu.au/issue37/davies_hartono.htm

De Dios, Aurora Javate (1999). Hidden No More: Violence against Women in the Philippines. In Fanny M. Cheung, Malavia Karlekar, Aurora de Dios, Juree Vichit-Vadakan and Lourdes R. Quisumbing (eds.), *Breaking the Silence: Violence Against Women in Asia*. Hong Kong: Equal Opportunities Commission, Women in Asia Development and UNESCO National Commisson on the Philippines, pp. 152–73.

De Jesus, Emerciana (2003). Interview with author, Quezon City, July 25.

Derichs, Claudia (2013). Reformasi and Repression: Wan Azizah Wan Ismail. In Claudia Derichs and Mark T. Thompson (eds.), *Dynasties and Female Political Leaders in Asia: Gender, Power and Pedigree*. Münster: Lit Verlag, pp. 291–320.

Derichs, Claudia and Thompson, Mark T. (eds.) (2013). *Dynasties and Female Political Leaders in Asia: Gender, Power and Pedigree*. Münster: Lit Verlag.

Devasahayam, Theresa (ed.) (2019). *Women and Politics in Southeast Asia: Navigating a Man's World*. Brighton: Sussex Academic Press.

Dewi, Kurniawati Hastuti (2015). *Indonesian Women and Local Politics: Islam, Gender and Networks in Post-Suharto Indonesia*. Singapore: National University of Singapore Press.

Downing, Sonja Lynn (2019). *Gamelan Girls. Gender, Childhood, and Politics in Balinese Music Ensembles*. Urbana: University of Illinois Press.

Drummond, Lisa (2004). The Modern "Vietnamese Woman": Socialization and Women's Magazines. In Lisa Drummond and Helle Rydstrom (eds.), *Gender Practices in Contemporary Vietnam*. Copenhagen: Nordic Institute of Asian Studies Press, pp. 158–78.

Earl, Catherine (2014). *Vietnam's New Middle Classes: Gender, Career, City*. Copenhagen: Nordic Institute of Asian Studies Press.

Edwards, Louise and Roces, Mina (2004). *Women's Suffrage in Asia: Gender, Nationalism and Democracy*. London: Routledge.

Endres, Kirsten W. (2011). *Performing the Divine: Mediums, Markets and Modernity in Urban Vietnam*. Copenhagen: Nordic Institute of Asian Studies Press.

Errington, Shelly (1990). Recasting Sex, Gender, and Power: A Theoretical and Regional Overview. In Jane Monnig Atkinson and Shelly Errington (eds.), *Power and Difference: Gender in Island Southeast Asia*. Stanford, CA: Stanford University Press, pp. 41–53.

Estrada-Claudio, Sylvia (2002). *Rape, Love and Sexuality: The Construction of Woman in Discourse*. Quezon City: University of the Philippines Press.

Fabella, Virginia (MM) (1987, 1991). Mission of Women in the Church in Asia: Role and Position. In Mary John Mananzan (ed.), *Essays on Women*. Manila: Institute of Women's Studies, pp.159–70.

Fahey, Stefanie (1998). Vietnam's Women in the Renovation Era. In Krishna Sen and Maila Stivens (eds.), *Gender and Power in Affluent Asia*. London: Routledge, pp.222–49.

Falk, Monica Lindberg (2010). Feminism, Buddhism and Transnational Women's Movements in Thailand. In Mina Roces and Louise Edwards (eds.), *Women's Movements in Asia: Feminisms and Transnational Activism*. London: Routledge, pp. 110–23.

Falk, Monica Lindberg (2007). *Making Fields of Merit: Buddhist Female Ascetics and Gendered Orders in Thailand*. Copenhagen: NationalNordic Institute of Asian Studies Press.

Ford, Michele and Lyons, Lenore (eds.) (2011). *Men and Masculinities in Southeast Asia*. London: Routledge.

Ford, Michele and Parker, Lyn (eds.) (2008). *Women and Work in Indonesia*. London: Routledge.

Frieson, Kate (2001). *In the Shadows: Women, Power and Politics in Cambodia*. Occasional Paper No. 26. Victoria, BC: Centre for Asia-Pacific Initiatives.

Frisk, Sylvia (2009). *Submitting to God: Women and Islam in Urban Malaysia*. Seattle: University of Washington Press.

Garcellano, Rosario, Lolarga, Elizabeth and Sarabia, Anna Leah (eds.) (1992). *Sisterhood is Global: Dialogues in the Philippines*. Quezon City: Circle Publications.

Garcia, Neil C. (2021). Philippine Gay Culture: An Update and a Postcolonial Autocritique. In Richard Chu and Mark Blasius (eds.), *More Tomboy and Bakla than We Admit*. Manila: Academia Filipina.

Garcia, Neil C. (1996). *Philippine Gay Culture: The Last Thirty Years Binabae to Bakla, Silahis to MSM*. Quezon City: University of the Philippines Press, pp. 52–85.

Gloria, Glenda and Danguilan-Vitug, Marites (1993). Socialite Seeking Legitimacy. *Philippine Daily Inquirer*, October 12, pp. 1, 10.

Harriden, Jessica (2012). *The Authority of Influence: Women and Power in Burmese History*. Copenhagen: Nordic Institute of Asian Studies Press.

Hefner, Claire (2019). On Fun and Freedom: Young Women's Moral Learning in Islamic Boarding Schools. *Journal of the Royal Anthropological Institute*, 25(3), 487–505.

Hilman, Ben (2017). Increasing Women's Parliamentary Representation in Asia and the Pacific: The Indonesian Experience. *Asia & the Pacific Policy Studies*, 4(1), 38–49.

Hoang, Lan Anh (2020). Vietnam's Women's Union and Contradictions of a Socialist Gender Regime. *Asian Studies Review*, 44(2), 297–314.

Hoang, Lan Anh and Yeoh, Brenda (2011). Breadwinning Wives and "Left-Behind" Husbands: Men and Masculinities in the Vietnamese Transnational Family. *Gender & Society*, 25(6),717–39.

Hoefinger, Heidi, Ly, Pisey Ly and Srun, Srorn (2016). Sex Politics and Moral Panics: LGBT Communities, Sex/Entertainment Workers and Sexually Active Youth in Cambodia. In Katherine Bricknell and Simon Springer (eds.), *The Handbook of Contemporary Cambodia*. London: Routledge, pp. 315–25.

hui, tan beng (2019). The LGBT Quandary in New Malaysia. *Australian Journal of Asian Law*, 20(1), pp. 197–212.

Ikeya, Chie (2014). Masculinities in Asia: A Review Essay. *Asian Studies Review*, 38(2), 243–52.

Ikeya, Chie (2011). *Refiguring Women, Colonialism and Modernity in Burma*. Honolulu: University of Hawaii Press.

Iwanaga, Kazuki (2008). Introduction: Women's Political Participation from an International Perspective. In Kazuki Iwanaga (ed.), *Women and Politics in Thailand*. Copenhagen:Nordic Institute of Asian Studies Press, pp.1–26.

Jackson, Peter A. (2011). Bangkok's Early Twenty-First-Century Queer Boom. In Peter A. Jackson (ed.), *Queer Bangkok: Twenty-First Century Markets, Media and Rights*. Hong Kong: Hong Kong University Press, pp. 17–42.

Jackson, Peter A. (1995). *Dear Uncle Go: Male Homosexuality in Thailand*. Bangkok: Bua Luang Books.

Jackson, Peter A. and Sullivan, Gerard (1999). A Panoply of Roles: Sexual and Gender Diversity in Contemporary Thailand. In Peter A. Jackson and Gerard Sullivan (eds.), *Lady Boys, Tom Boys, Rent Boys: Male and Female Homosexualities in Contemporary Thailand*. New York: The Hamworth Press, pp.1–27.

Jackson, Peter and Cook, Nerida (1999). *Gender and Sexualities in Modern Thailand*. Chiang Mai: Silkworm Books.

Jacobsen, Trude (2011). Being Broh: The Good, the Bad and the Successful Man in Cambodia. In Michele Ford and Lenore Lyons (eds.), *Men and Masculinities in Southeast Asia*. London: Routledge, pp. 86–102.

Jacobsen, Trudy (2010). Riding a Buffalo to Cross a Muddy Field: Heuristic Approaches to Feminism in Cambodia. In Mina Roces and Louise Edwards (eds.), *Women's Movements in Asia: Feminisms and Transnational Activism*. London: Routledge, pp. 207–23.

Jacobsen, Trudy (2008). *Lost Goddesses: The Denial of Power in Cambodian History*. Copenhagen: Nordic Institute of Asian Studies Press.

Jeffrey, Leslie Ann (2001). *Sex and Borders: Gender, National Identity and Prostitution Policy in Thailand*. Vancouver, BC: University of British Columbia Press.

Johnson, Mark (1997). *Beauty and Power: Transgendering and Cultural Transformation in the Southern Philippines*. London: Routledge.

Joseph, Cynthia (2014). *Growing Up Female in Multi-Ethnic Malaysia*. London: Routledge.

Kabullah, Muhammad Ichsan and Fajri, M. Nurul (2021). Neo-Ibuism in Indonesian Politics: Election Campaigns of Wives of Regional Heads in West Sumatra in 2019. *Journal of Current Southeast Asian Affairs*, 60(1), 136–55.

Kawanami, Hiroko (2013). *Renunciation and Empowerment of Buddhist Nuns in Myanmar-Burma*. Leiden: Brill.

Keeler, Ward (2017). *The Traffic in Hierarchy: Masculinity and Its Others in Buddhist Burma*. Honolulu: University of Hawaii Press.

Keyes, Charles F. (1984). Mother or Mistress but Never a Monk: Buddhist Notions of Female Gender in Rural Thailand. *American Ethnologist*, 11(2), 223–41.

Kloos, David (2019). Experts Beyond Discourse: Women, Islamic Authority, and the Performance of Professionalism in Malaysia. *American Ethnologist*, 46(2), 162–75.

Kyi, Aung San Suu (1995). *Freedom from Fear and Other Writings*. London: Penguin.

Kyi, Ma Khin Mar Mar (2018). Gender. In Adam Simpson, Nicholas Farrelly and Ian Holliday (eds.), *Routledge Handbook of Contemporary Myanmar*. London: Routledge, pp. 381–90.

Lan, Pie-Chia (2006). *Global Cinderellas: Migrant Domestics and Newly Rich Employers in Taiwan*. Durham, NC: Duke University Press.

Ledgerwood, Judy (1996). Politics and Gender: Negotiating Conceptions of the Ideal Woman in Present Day Cambodia. *Asia Pacific Viewpoint*, 37(2), 139–52.

Lee, Julian C. H. (2018). *Women's Activism in Malaysia: Voices and Insights*. London: Palgrave Macmillan.

Lee, Julian C. H. (2012). Sexuality Rights Activism in Malaysia: The Case of Seksualiti Merdeka. In Michele Ford (ed.), *Social Activism in Southeast Asia*. London: Routledge, pp. 170–86.

Leong, Lawrence Wai-Teng (2012). Asian Sexuality or Singapore Exceptionalism? *Liverpool Law Review*, 33, 11–26.

Leshkowich, Ann Marie (2014). *Essential Trade: Vietnamese Women in a Changing Marketplace*. Honolulu: University of Hawaii Press.

Lowe, Viviane (1994). Women in Arms: Representations of Vietnamese Women at War 1965–1975. Paper presented to the Workshop on Southeast Asian Women, Monash University.

Lyons, Lenore (2010). Transnational Networks and Localized Campaigns: The Women's Movement in Singapore. In Mina Roces and Louise Edwards (eds.), *Women's Movements in Asia: Feminisms and Transnational Activism*. London: Routledge, pp. 75–89.

Lyons, Lenore (2004). *A State of Ambivalence: The Feminist Movement in Singapore*. Leiden: Brill.

Maber, Elizabeth J. T. and Pyo Let Han (2018). Challenging Gender Inequalities Through Education and Activism: Exploring the Work of Women's Organizations in Myanmar's Transition. In Mehrangiz Najafizadeh and Linda Lindsey (eds.), *Women of Asia: Globalization, Development and Gender Equity*. London: Routledge, pp.268–80.

Mahey, Petra, Winarita, Monica Swasti and Herriman, Nicholas (2016). Presumptions of Promiscuity: Reflections on Being a Widow or Divorcee from Three Indonesian Communities. *Indonesia and the Malay World*, 44 (128), 47–67.

Manalansan IV, Martin F. (2006). *Global Divas: Filipino Gay Men in the Diaspora*. Quezon City: Ateneo de Manila University Press.

Mananzan, Mary John (OSB) (1994). Theological Perspectives of a Religious Woman Today – Four Trends of Emerging Spirituality. In Ursula King (ed.), *Feminist Theology in the Third World*. New York: Orbis Press, pp.340–49.

Mananzan, Mary John (OSB) (1987). The Filipino Woman Before and After the Spanish Conquest of the Philippines. In Mary John Mananzan (ed.), *Essays on Women*, revised edn. Manila: Institute of Women's Studies, pp. 6–35.

Manapat, Ricardo (1991). *Some Are Smarter Than Others: The History of Marcos's Crony Capitalism*. New York: Aletheia Publications.

Mangahas, Fe and Llaguno, Jenny R. (eds.) (2006). *Centennial Crossings: Readings on Babaylan Feminism in the Philippines*. Quezon City: C & E Publishing.

Martyn, Elizabeth (2005). *The Women's Movement in Postcolonial Indonesia: Gender and Nation in a New Democracy*. London: Routledge.

McKay, Stephen (2007). Filipino Sea Men: Identity, Masculinity in a Global Labour Niche. In Rhacel Parreñas and Lok C. D. Siu (eds.), *Asian Diasporas: New Formations, New Conceptions*. Stanford, CA: Stanford University Press, pp. 63–83.

Mckay, Stephen and Lucero-Prismo III, Don Eliseo (2012). Masculinities Afloat: Filipino Seafarers and the Situational Performance of Manhood. In Michele Ford and Lenore Lyons (eds.), *Men and Masculinities in Southeast Asia*. London: Routledge, pp.20–37.

Mijares, Primitovo (1976). *The Conjugal Dictatorship of Ferdinand and Imelda Marcos*. New York: Union Square Publications.

Mikkelsen, Henrik Hvenegaard (2018). *Cutting Cosmos: Masculinity and Spectacular Events among the Bugkalot*. New York: Berghahn Books.

Muntarbhorn, Vitit (2020). Thailand's Same-Sex Civil Partnership Law – A Rainbow Trailblazer? *East Asia Forum*, September 2. www.eastasia

forum.org/2020/09/02/thailands-same-sex-civil-partnership-law-a-rainbow-trailblazer/.

Murray, Alison J. (1991). *No Money, No Honey: A Study of Street Traders and Prostitutes in Jakarta*. Singapore: Oxford University Press.

Murtagh, Ben (2013). *Genders and Sexualities in Indonesian Cinema: Constructing Gay, Lesbi and Waria Identities on Screen*. London: Routledge.

Ng, Cecilia, Mohamad, Maznah and hui, tan beng (2006). *Feminism and the Women's Movement in Malaysia: An Unsung (R)evolution*. London: Routledge.

Ng, Eve (2018). LGBT Advocacy and Transnational Funding in Singapore and Malaysia. *Development and Change*, 49(4), 1093–1114.

Niner, Sara (2016). *Women and the Politics of Gender in Post-Conflict Timor-Leste: Between Heaven and Earth*. London: Routledge.

Nurmila, Nina (2009). *Women, Islam and Everyday Life: Negotiating Polygamy in Indonesia*. London: Routledge.

Ong, Aihwa (1987). *Spirits of Resistance and Capitalist Discipline: Factory Women in Malaysia*. Albany, NY: SUNY University Press.

Ong, Aihwa and Peletz, Michael (eds.) (1995). *Bewitching Women, Pious Men, Gender and Body Politics in Southeast Asia*. Berkeley: University of California Press.

O'Shaughnessy (2009). *Gender, State and Social Power in Contemporary Indonesia: Divorce and Marriage Law*. London: Routledge.

Parker, Lyn (2008). Theorising Adolescent Sexualities in Indonesia—Where "Something Different Happens". *Intersections*, 18. http://intersections.anu.edu.au/issue18/parker.htm.

Parker, Lyn and Nilan, Pam (2013). *Adolescents in Contemporary Indonesia*. London: Routledge.

Parker, Lyn, Riyani, Irma and Nolan, Brooke (2016). The Stigmatisation of Widows and Divorcees (*janda*) in Indonesia, and the Possibilities of Agency. *Indonesia and the Malay World*, 44(128), 27–46.

Parreñas, Rhacel (2005). *Children of Global Migration: Transnational Families and Gendered Woes*. Quezon City: Ateneo de Manila University Press.

Parreñas, Rhacel (2001). *Servants of Globalization: Women, Migration and Domestic Work*. Quezon City: Ateneo de Manila University Press.

Peletz, Michael (2012). Gender, Sexuality and the State in Southeast Asia. *The Journal of Asian Studies*, 71(4), 895–917.

Peletz, Michael (2006). Transgenderism and Gender Pluralism in Southeast Asia Since Early Modern Times. *Current Anthropology*, 47(2), 309–40.

Peletz, Michael (1996). *Reason and Passion: Representations of Gender in Malay Society*. Berkeley: University of California Press.

Peletz, Michael (1995). Neither Reasonable or Responsible: Contrasting Representations of Masculinity in Malay Society. In Aihwa Ong and Michael G. Peletz (eds.), *Bewitching Women, Pious Men: Gender and Body Politics in Southeast Asia*. Berkeley: University of California Press, pp. 70–106.

Peters, Robbie (2016). Single Working-Class Women and the City in Java and Vietnam. *Asian Studies Review*, 40(1), 36–52.

Pettus, Ashley (2003). *Between Sacrifice and Desire: National Identity and the Governing of Femininity in Vietnam*. London: Routledge.

Philipps, Robert (2014). "And I Am Also Gay": Illiberal Pragmatics, Neoliberal Homonormativity and LGBT Activism in Singapore. *Anthropologica*, 56(1), 45–54.

Pierskalla, Jan H., Lauretig, Adam, Rosenberg, Andrew S. and Sacks, Audrey (2021). Democratization and Representative Bureaucracy: An Analysis of Promotion Patterns in Indonesia's Civil Service, 1980–2015. *American Journal of Political Science*, 65(2), pp. 261–77.

Pingol, Alice Tadeo (2001). *Remaking Masculinities: Identity, Power and Gender Dynamics in Families with Migrant Wives and Househusbands*. Quezon City: University of the Philippines Press.

Platt, Maria (2017). *Marriage, Gender and Islam in Indonesia: Women Negotiating Informal Marriage, Divorce and Desire*. London: Routledge.

Resurrección, Bernadette (1999). *Transforming Nature, Redefining Selves: Gender and Ethnic Relations, Resource Use, and Environmental Change in the Philippine Uplands*. Maastricht: Shaker Publishing.

Reyes, Raquel A. G. (2008). *Love, Passion and Patriotism: Sexuality and the Philippine Propaganda Movement, 1882–1892*. Singapore: National University of Singapore Press.

Reyes, Raquel A. G. and Clarence-Smith, William G. (eds.) (2012). *Sexual Diversity in Asia, c. 600–1959*. London: Routledge.

Rinaldo, Rachel (2013). *Mobilizing Piety: Islam and Feminism in Indonesia*. Oxford: Oxford University Press.

Robinson, Kathryn (2018). Gender and Politics in Post-New Order Indonesia. In Robert Hefner (ed.), *Routledge Handbook of Contemporary Indonesia*. London: Routledge, pp. 309–21.

Robinson, Kathryn (2014). Masculinity, Sexuality and Islam: The Gender Politics of Regime Change in Indonesia. In Linda Rae Bennett and Sharyn Graham Davies (eds.), *Sex and Sexualities in Contemporary Indonesia: Sexual Politics, Health, Diversity and Representations*. London: Routledge, pp. 51–68.

Robinson, Kathryn (2008). *Gender, Islam and Democracy in Indonesia*. London: Routledge.

Roces, Mina (2021). *The Filipino Migration Experience: Global Agents of Change*. Ithaca, NY: Cornell University Press.

Roces, Mina (2012). *Women's Movements and the Filipina, 1986–2008*. Honolulu: University of Hawaii Press.

Roces, Mina (2010). Asian Feminisms: Women's Movements from the Asian Perspective. In Mina Roces and Louise Edwards (eds.), *Women's Movements in Asia: Feminisms and Transnational Activism*. London: Routledge, pp. 1–20.

Roces, Mina (1998). *Women, Power and Kinship Politics: Female Power in Post-War Philippines*. Westport, CT: Praeger.

Roces, Mina and Edwards, Louise (eds.) (2010). *Women's Movements in Asia: Feminisms and Transnational Activism*. London: Routledge.

Rodriguez, Evelyn Ibatan (2012). *Celebrating Debutantes and Quinceñeras: Coming of Age in American Ethnic Communities*. Philadelphia, PA: Temple University Press.

Roxas, Judy (1995). Interview with author, Quezon City, February 7.

Rydstrom, Helle (1998). *Embodying Morality. Girls' Socialization in a North Vietnamese Commune*. Linkoping: Department of Gender Studies, Linkoping University.

Sandy, Larissa (2014). *Women and Sex Work in Cambodia: Blood, Sweat and Tears*. London: Routledge,.

Satriyo, Hana A. (2010). Pushing the Boundaries: Women in Direct Local Elections and Local Government. In Edward Aspinall and Marcus Mietzer (eds.), *Problems of Democratisation in Indonesia: Elections, Institutions and Society*. Singapore: Institute of Southeast Asian Studies Publishing, pp.243–63.

Schuler, Sidney Ruth, Hoang, Tu Anh, Ha, Vu Song Ha, Tran, Hung Minh, Bui, Thi Than Mai and Thien, Pham Vu (2006). Constructions of Gender in Vietnam: In Pursuit of the Three Criteria. *Culture, Health and Sexuality*, 8(5), pp. 383–94.

Sears, Laurie J. (ed.) (1996). Fragile Identities: Deconstructing Women and Indonesia. In Laurie J. Sears (ed.), *Fantasizing the Feminine in Indonesia*. Durham, NC: Duke University Press, pp. 1–44.

Sen, Krishna and Stivens, Maila (1998). *Gender and Power in Affluent Asia*. London: Routledge.

Sheehy, Grace, Yadanar, Aung and Foster, Angel M. (2015). "We Can Lose Our Life for the Abortion": Exploring the Dynamics Shaping Abortion Care in Peri-Urban Yangon, Myanmar. *Contraception*, 92(5), pp. 475–81.

Sim, Amy (2010). Lesbianism among Indonesian Migrants in Hong Kong. In Yau Ching (ed.), *As Normal as Possible*. Hong Kong: Hong Kong University Press, pp.37–50.

Yahoo! News Editorial Team (2021). Singapore's Apex Court Hears Challenges to Law Criminalising Sex Between Men. *Yahoo! News*. January 26. https://sg .news.yahoo.com/singapores-apex-court-law-criminalising-sex-between-men-010805158.html?guccounter=1. Accessed February 22, 2021.

Sinnott, Megan (2011). The Language of Rights, Deviance and Pleasure: Organizational Responses to Discourses of Same-Sex Sexuality and Transgenderism in Thailand. In Peter A. Jackson (ed.), *Queer Bangkok: Twenty-First Century Markets, Media and Rights*. Hong Kong: Hong Kong University Press, pp. 205–24.

Sinnott, Megan (2004). *Toms and Dees: Transgender Identity and Same-Sex Relationships in Thailand*. Honolulu: University of Hawaii Press.

Smith, Bianca J. (2014). When Wahyu Comes Through Women: Female Spiritual Authority and Divine Revelation in Mystical Groups and Pesantren-Sufi Orders. In Bianca J. Smith and Mark Woodwards (eds.), *Gender and Power in Indonesian Islam: Leaders, Feminists and Pesantren Selves*. London: Routledge, pp. 83–102.

Smith, Bianca J. and Woodward, Mark (eds.) (2014). *Gender and Power in Indonesian Islam: Leaders, Feminists and Pesantren Selves*. London: Routledge.

Smith, Bianca J. and Woodward, Mark (2014). Introduction: De-Colonizing Islam and Muslim Feminism. In Bianca J. Smith and Mark Woodward (eds.), *Gender and Power in Indonesian Islam: Leaders, Feminists and Pesantren Selves*. London: Routledge, pp.1–21.

Smith-Hefner, Nancy (2019). *Islamizing Intimacies: Youth, Sexuality and Gender in Contemporary Indonesia*. Honolulu: University of Hawaii Press.

Smith-Hefner, Nancy (2018). From Soft Patriarch to Companionate Partner: Muslim Masculinity in Java since the "New Order." In Marcia C. Inhorn and Nefissa Naguib (eds.), *Reconceiving Muslim Men. Love and Marriage, Family and Care in Precarious Times*. New York: Berghahn Books, pp. 85–106.

Stivens, Maila (1996). *Matriliny and Modernity: Sexual Politics and Social Change in Rural Malaysia*. St. Leonards: Allen & Unwin.

Stivens, Maila (1991). Why Gender Matters in Southeast Asian Politics. In Maila Stivens (ed.), *Why Gender Matters in Southeast Asian Politics*. Clayton, VA: Monash Papers on Southeast Asia No. 23, pp. 9–24.

Stivens, Maila and Sen, Krishna (1998). *Gender and Power in Affluent Asia*. London: Routledge.

Suryakusuma, Julia (1996). The State and Sexuality in New Order Indonesia. In Laurie J. Sears (ed.), *Fantasizing the Feminine in Indonesia*. Durham, NC: Duke University Press, pp. 92–119.

Tang, Shawna (2017). *Postcolonial Lesbian Identities in Singapore: Re-thinking Global Sexualities*. London: Routledge.

Tapales, Proserpina D. (2002). Engendering Local Governance. *Review of Women's Studies*, 12(1&2), 49–62.

Taylor, Jean Gelman (ed.) (1997). *Women Creating Indonesia: The First Fifty Years*. Clayton, VA: Monash Asia Institute.

Teik, Pang Khee (2014). *Sexual Citizenship in Conflict*. In Meredith Weiss (ed.), *Routledge Handbook of Contemporary Malaysia*. London: Routledge, pp. 361–73.

Torres, Amaryllis Tiglao (2002). *Love in the Time of Ina Morata*. Quezon City: University of the Philippines Center for Women's Studies.

Ungar, Esta (2000). Re-gendering Vietnam: From Militant to Market Socialism. In Louise Edwards and Mina Roces (eds.), *Women in Asia: Tradition, Modernity and Globalisation*. Sydney: Allen & Unwin, pp. 291–317.

Ungar, Esta (1994). Gender, Land and Household in Vietnam. *Asian Studies Review*, 17(3), 61–72.

Van Wichelen, Sonja (2010). *Religion, Politics and Gender in Indonesia: Disputing the Muslim Body*. London: Routledge.

Van Wijngaarden, Jan W. De Lind (1999). Between Money, Morality and Masculinity: Bar-Based Male Sex Work in Chiang Mai. In Peter A. Jackson and Gerard Sullivan (eds.), *Lady Boys, Tom Boys, Rent Boys: Male and Male Homosexualities in Contemporary Thailand*. New York: The Haworth Press, pp. 193–218.

Wardani, Sri Budi Eko and Subekti, Valina Singka (2021). Political Dynasties and Women Candidates in Indonesia's 2019 Election. *Journal of Current Southeast Asian Affairs*, 40(1), 28–49.

Weiss, Meredith L. (2013). Prejudice Before Pride: Rise of an Anticipatory Countermovement. In Meredith L. Weiss and Michael J. Bosia (eds.), *Global Homophobia: States, Movements, and the Politics of Oppression*. Champaign: University of Illinois Press, pp. 149–73.

Weiss, Meredith L. (2007). "We Know Who You Are. We'll Employ You": Non-Discrimination and Singapore's Bohemian Dreams. In M. V. Lee Badgett and Jeff Frank (eds.), *Sexual Orientation Discrimination: An International Perspective*. London: Routledge, pp. 164–76.

Werner, Jayne (2009). *Gender, Household and State in Post-Revolutionary Vietnam*. London: Routledge.

Werner, Jayne and Bélanger, Danièle (eds.) (2002). *Gender, Household and State: Doi Moi in Vietnam*. Ithaca, NY: Cornell University Southeast Asia Program Publications.

Whittaker, Andrea (2000). *Intimate Knowledge. Women and Their Health in North-East Thailand*. St. Leonards: Allen & Unwin.

Whittaker, Andrea (2004). *Abortion, Sin and the State in Thailand*. London: Routledge.

Wieringa, Saskia (2021). Gay Couple Caned in Aceh, Indonesia. *People's Charter for Southeast Asia*. February 7. https://forsea.co/gay-couple-caned-in-aceh-indonesia/. Accessed March 3, 2021.

Wieringa, Saskia (2019). Is the Recent Wave of Homophobia in Indonesia Unexpected? In Greg Fealy and Ronit Ricci (eds.), *Contentious Belonging: The Place of Minorities in Indonesia*. Singapore: Institute of Southeast Asian Studies Publishing, pp. 113–32.

Wieringa, Saskia (2015). Gender Harmony and the Happy Family: Islam, Gender and Sexuality in Post-Reformasi Indonesia. *Journal of South East Asian Research*, 23(1), 27–44.

Wieringa, Saskia (2002). *Sexual Politics in Indonesia*. Houndmills: Palgrave Macmillan.

Wieringa, Saskia, with Bhaiya, Abha and Katjasungkana, Nursyahbani (2015). *Heteronormativity, Passionate Aesthetics and Symbolic Subversion in Asia*. Brighton: Sussex Academic Press.

Wijaya, Hendri Yulius (2020). *Intimate Assemblages: The Politics of Queer Identities and Sexualities in Indonesia*. Singapore: Springer.

Wijaya, Hendri Yulius and Davies, Sharyn Graham (2019). The Unfulfilled Promise of Democracy: Lesbian and Gay Activism in Indonesia. In Thushara Dibley and Michele Ford (eds.), *Activists in Transition Progressive Politics in Democratic Indonesia*. Ithaca, NY: Cornell University Press, pp.153–70.

Williams, Louise (2001). *Wives, Mistresses and Matriarchs: Asian Women Today*. London: Phoenix Press.

Wilson, Ara (2004). *The Intimate Economies of Bangkok: Tomboys, Tycoons, and Avon Ladies in the Global City*. Berkeley: University of California Press.

Wolf, Diane Lauren (1992). *Factory Daughters: Gender, Household Dynamics and Rural Industrialization in Java*. Berkeley: University of California Press.

Yue, Audrey, Leung, Helen Hok-Sze, Collins, Alan, Gorman-Murray, Andrew and Hubbard, Phil (2017). Notes Towards the Queer Asian City: Singapore and Hong Kong. *Urban Studies*, 54(3), 747–64.

Yulius, Hendri, Tang, Shawna and Offord, Baden (2018). The Globalization of LGBT Identity and Same-Sex Marriage as a Catalyst of Neo-Institutional Values: Singapore and Indonesia in Focus. In Browyn Winter, Maxime Forest and Réjane Sénac (eds.), *Global Perspectives on Same-Sex Marriage: A Neo-institutional Approach*. London: Springer, pp. 171–96.

Cambridge Elements ≡

Politics and Society in Southeast Asia

Edward Aspinall

Australian National University

Edward Aspinall is a professor of politics at the Coral Bell School of Asia-Pacific Affairs, Australian National University. A specialist of Southeast Asia, especially Indonesia, much of his research has focused on democratisation, ethnic politics and civil society in Indonesia and, most recently, clientelism across Southeast Asia.

Meredith L. Weiss

University at Albany, SUNY

Meredith L. Weiss is Professor of Political Science at the University at Albany, SUNY. Her research addresses political mobilization and contention, the politics of identity and development, and electoral politics in Southeast Asia, with particular focus on Malaysia and Singapore.

About the Series

The Elements series Politics and Society in Southeast Asia includes both country-specific and thematic studies on one of the world's most dynamic regions. Each title, written by a leading scholar of that country or theme, combines a succinct, comprehensive, up-to-date overview of debates in the scholarly literature with original analysis and a clear argument.

Cambridge Elements ☰

Politics and Society in Southeast Asia

Elements in the Series

A full series listing is available at: www.cambridge.org/ESEA

Printed in the United States
by Baker & Taylor Publisher Services